THE ART OF
LO BAN PAI

AN INTRODUCTION TO
THE INTERNAL PHILOSOPHY
OF SPIRAL ENERGETICS

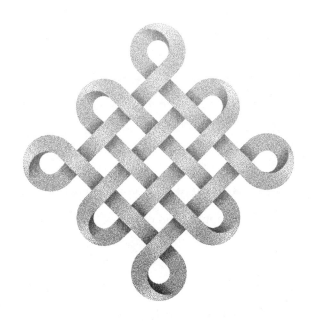

LUJAN MATUS

DISCLAIMER

ISBN: 9781657682726

With deepest gratitude

To Naomi Jean

for your dedication and devotion all these years.

Editing, formatting, cover art, adaptation of the Lo Ban Pai
Hunab Ku, design layout and synopses by Naomi Jean.

www.parallelperception.com

ACKNOWLEDGEMENTS

Thank you to David Bernard⁺ for your beautiful work in the
creation of the new Parallel Perception website, adaptation
of cover graphic and program insignia for this book.

Thank you to Kory Matthew for your loving devotion
and input in my life and for writing the introduction:
'Welcome to the Art of Lo Ban Pai'.

⁺BMUSED Imaging Graphics and Web Design, bmusedimaging.com

NOTE TO THE READER

This book is a compilation of material from the Parallel Perception website describing the art of Lo Ban Pai and the various programs offered by Lujan Matus. It was created on the request of Lujan's students to have the information available in a readily accessible format.

Table of Contents

WELCOME TO
THE ART OF LO BAN PAI

This handbook outlines the essential elements of Lo Ban Pai as a philosophy, along with a complete overview of all the programs available to be undertaken under the guidance of Lujan Matus.

www.parallelperception.com

If you have found this book, you are ready to take a major step forward within your own spiritual journey. Lujan's students typically are those who have been searching for something much more than the commonly available, who take responsibility for their own development and who seek the eminently practical and powerful that encompasses the magical and mystical that surrounds us.

Within our living construct is an all-embracing consciousness that awaits our sincere gestures to establish contact with it. Everybody is seeking that communion. The movements within Lo Ban Pai provide an astonishingly fast connection with the unknown which often shocks practitioners with its immediacy. The feelings of gravity and magnetism that arrive in one's hands become obvious after only a few moments under Lujan's tutelage, and will provide you with an endlessly renewing source of inspiration to continue upon your journey.

Lo Ban Pai goes beyond the system of movements, encompassing also the teachings of Lujan Matus. Within Lujan's writings are incredible amounts of information that will assist you in gaining access to your internal vortices and thus awaken you to your own personal power. These books invite you to read them again and again, each time revealing greater depth in accordance with your own progression, taking you yet further forward.

When you undertake tuition, you will directly discover the world of the intuitive empath and learn to alter the intimate details of your timeline, beyond the present engineered consciousness.

You will be gently shown the interferences that are part of the socially conditioned response of many individuals living upon this planet, which may be blocking you from being who you really are. This will empower you to move toward the purest form of your predetermined life path.

If you are wondering how Lo Ban Pai can affect such profound changes within your life, we invite you to explore the multitude of testimonials from Lujan's students that can be found on the Parallel Perception website. On the front page of the site you will also find an outline of some of the

www.parallelperception.com

manifest benefits you are likely to experience, which are worth repeating here.

Lo Ban Pai will help you:

- Increase your energy

- Cultivate personal power

- Awaken heart consciousness

- Access your third eye capacity

- Promote optimal health and vitality

- Improve muscle strength and flexibility

- Experience heightened states of awareness

It is a unique coiling system that applies the golden ratio spiral principles of the Tao.

Welcome to what you have been looking for.

"The love that you withhold is the pain that you carry"

Ralph Waldo Emerson

ELEGANTLY FLOURISHING SPIRALS

Lo Ban Pai is a comprehensive art that enlivens reservoirs of empathic communion through movements that inspire feelings of heartfelt gratitude. This in turn manifests a true internal standpoint of personal power that brings a genuine ethical view to the forefront of the witness. Comprised of elegant movement sequences and profound awareness techniques with a deeply meditative core, Lo Ban Pai recalibrates perception away from a socially engineered mindset and towards a heart-based approach.

Translated as elegantly flourishing spirals, Lo Ban aptly describes the signature coiling motions of the movement family, and Pai indicates a dynamic hand or fist. This name was

1

given to the system by the intuitive empath Lujan Matus in honor of his benefactor, Lo Ban, a prodigious warrior seer from the Altai-Sayan region of central Asia. As an Oriental shaman, he traveled very deeply into the essence of the Tao, meaning The Way (of doing and being).

Lo Ban Pai operates in harmony with the guiding laws of nature, generating toroidal vortices within and around the body. Mirroring the Fibonacci principle, its unique coiling gestures open up energetic whirlpools, or shen gongs, which avail one to heightened levels of sensitivity towards the subtleties of the surrounding world. This photonic light energy is automatically absorbed into these etheric portals and it is this direct interactivity that delivers the deepest mysteries of Lo Ban Pai to the one who practices.

DOORWAY TO THE TAO

Doorway to the Tao refers to an etheric entry point to the emptiness that reveals everything, which is a simple means to traverse the complexity of the unknown. Lo Ban Pai draws us into the locus of what is arriving upon us naturally in terms of our own evolutionary process of awakening. The movements are the physical recipe that opens up that gateway into an intention-less state that holds volumes of sensory data. This is the living application of the Tao.

Simultaneously expressing both formlessness and form, Lo Ban Pai is characterized by adaptive fluidity and a primary emphasis upon heart alignment. Entering into this system necessitates a sincere engagement and ultimately beckons a

3

humble stance of personal responsibility within the momentary circumstances one is immersed within. Every person, every moment, every gesture is a threshold.

When we perform Lo Ban Pai we become etherically connected to an intangible world. The figure-eight movements open up a field of supreme connectivity that is an empathic universal response to the pure gestures of the practitioner. What avails itself is not defined by the socially deemed world we are surrounded by. The practice effectively opens up a realm of holographic exchange that exists beyond such constructs. It is timeless. This is how the Tao becomes a tangible information base that is endlessly renewed.

We must realize that no spiritual practice of substance can be made concrete, for concreteness becomes a viable method of bias, which can only be turned into dogma as a belief system to be rigidly held. When we create shen gongs we unlock our fields of bias into a momentary experience of intangibility that contains so many possibilities.

This receptivity then has to be recalibrated into the practical points that allow us to move forward or not. We have to be immediate enough to realize what can be done and what cannot be done within the moments that arrive.

INTENTIONAL POWER THROUGH
THE MASTERY OF MOVEMENT

Personal power manifests itself as a physical feeling that can be applied within the gravity of a circumstance and only in relation with the variables we are momentarily contained within. Through being instructed in Lo Ban Pai one begins to locate the central point where personal power arises and learns to identify the subtle nuances that indicate when to act and when to withdraw.

The steadfast intentionality of one's physical routine cultivates power through cyclic movements that reveal themselves anew every time. By persevering through daily practice of Lo Ban Pai one may obtain deep wisdom as a result of being subject to the same thing from different perspectives. The body evolves into an alternate frequency each time one becomes immersed within the system.

We all have a central axis within our body in terms of our own determination, our own experience. Nevertheless, due to the spiraling factor of the Fibonacci principle, our journey will always locate us in an alternate position to where we had previously been.

As we shift into new non-identifiable zones of arrival we learn to remain fluidly available in response to the intangible essence of each moment, which escapes points of reference that create dogma or bias. In each emerging vantage point we are seeing things from a totally different perspective, and we can't really expect to find what we will discover. It discovers us. If we don't gratify ourself by thinking we have found something, wisdom arrives.

VITALITY, WELL-BEING
AND PHOTONIC ENERGY

Lo Ban Pai instigates a profound realignment of the organic and energetic systems of the body through its natural spiral-based architecture. Deep harmonization of internal and external elements is established through the cellular resonance initiated via the signature coiling motions that increase light sensitivity, or the photonic potential, of the practitioner.

Lo Ban Pai movements support the body to function like a Tesla Coil, cultivating magnetic charge at the lower dantien, which builds and rises through the central matrix to the heart and third eye. This creates an internal energetic vortex that opens the central channels, which in turn strengthens the toroidal field around the body. Once sufficient energy has been generated it proliferates to bring the whole biofield into harmonic alignment and unravels physical, mental and emotional blockages. Personal transformation, healing and optimal states of well-being naturally follow once these conditions are in place.

An abundance of photonic power directly addresses key energy centers in the body, notably the lower dantien, heart, and third eye chakras. The lower dantien is the house of our primordial essence, known as Jing. The heart dantien houses our Chi: representing the manifestation of the power of movement and our capacity to act and be inspired.

The third eye, or Shen, has to do with holistic alignment and becoming aware of esoteric aspects of our beingness manifesting around us. Shen is enlivened in direct correspondence with our growth as a human being and its proliferation indicates the culmination of these three key elements all coming together as the sacred trinity of power itself.

Within the central matrix of our toroidal field our cells are autonomously synchronous; singularly aware yet attuned empathically to each other in terms of co-operation. Individual consciousness can be viewed in a parallel manner, as a worldwide anomaly that brings to light the cascade effect each awareness has, not only upon our own circumstances but upon the past, present and future of the collective whole.

DRAGON GATES

Dragon gates are the shen-gongs located within and surrounding the body that connect us to the world at large. Through processes of social engineering crucial aspects of their inherent functionality are muted. Lo Ban Pai reactivates these power centers so that dormant electromagnetic hubs return to their original state as the natural interdimensional portals that they are.

Unlike passive or still meditation that relies on abstract concepts such as mantra or rituals, Lo Ban Pai directly engages the etheric energy field and kinesthetic awareness, which then draws in situational attraction in terms of what we become open to. When our peripheral focus is placed on both activated palms, these two points form a hidden third location. This creates a refraction of attention, which allows the practitioner to locate and connect to the Dragon Gates in terms of feeling.

The dynamic application of movements and active mudras of Lo Ban Pai activate the shen-gongs as bi-directional portals. The practitioner beckons from within, and eternity finds an opening whereby it can respond. This manifests the subtle miracle of entering a Dragon Gate, which is a direct experience of communion with spirit, for one's emptiness co-opts an intimate interaction that is heart based. Once received the solar plexus then disseminates this impulse through the entire system. These gifts of eternity allow us to glean insights, even years after an event, as one's reality manifests situations relevant to our true evolution.

Within Lo Ban Pai, we generate vortices via the movements, which in essence allow us to apprehend all forms of light directly from our environment. These frequencies are inevitably transformed and collected by our toroidal field.

When we become electrically charged via our practice we create heightened sensitivity within our biofield and this enhances our capacity to absorb and then observe what is necessary for the evolution of our consciousness. Thus our body becomes familiarized with the omnipresent factor, which is fractally available and will adapt and facilitate accordingly to the needs of the moment.

Everything that is realized is readapted into each individual's bioelectromagnetic matrix. This is how we step forward into our own personal spiritual growth as conscious beings, in terms of attempting to be aware of what we are traveling towards.

The information that arrives upon our biofield through these dragon gates is always transforming, since our planet is traveling, the stars are moving and everything is in continual flux. We are subject to different light, alternative pressures and endless variations of frequency as a result of that perpetual motion.

The vortices created within Lo Ban Pai, through the elegant gestures of this internal system, are conjoined with figure-eight movements, which function as a key that unlocks the surrounding energy field. These dynamic mudras allow the unknown to become infused within our field of consciousness in terms of our capacity to understand what we are absorbing as feeling.

Feeling is a universal language that inevitably transforms into insight, then that frequency is adapted into the words that need to be spoken, and this arrival is like being subject to a different culture. Each time this influx renews, one becomes extremely expansive as a result of the frequential recalibration. By virtue of this contact one invariably evolves into the fractal anomaly that we truly are as interdimensional beings.

A PATH WITH HEART

The mastery of one's inner self is a heart path that realizes the internal essence of the arrival of everything within one's field of perception. Lo Ban Pai offers a uniquely practical method for activating this profound intelligence. One's heart hears and sees and doesn't speak to itself. It knows when to act and when to withdraw. It is courageous enough to openly verbalize a non-scripted truth and subtle enough to remain silent when appropriate.

To utter the scriptures of this internal awareness, which is the true mind, is to represent a mysterious source of intelligence that becomes viable through the voice of the person who has thus become its conduit.

Within this path of integrity, one must continually adapt and adjust, and this implies strategy. In this case strategies are not implemented.

Instead they are duly noted, and one becomes purposeful in terms of not applying what has been realized, allowing it to manifest as insight instead of a doing. Then it becomes transformed via the mysteries of emptiness into a not-doing.

The path thus revealed corresponds to the needs and the values of that particular person's realizations, and the growth of each individual is defined by where they are, not where they think they should be. Every step taken by every person is then revealed to be appropriate via their situational attunement, for the doorway that opens up will inevitably relate to the process of their own awakening.

LEARNING LO BAN PAI

Lo Ban Pai forms are taught during week-long programs, following a natural learning curve that builds essential skills from the foundation up. Students are fully equipped to apply the practices of each series once the course is completed. Lujan Matus is a master of engaging intuitively from an empathic perspective to access the most potent axis of transformation in any given circumstance. This means that what arrives naturally in terms of an evolutionary process of personal and collective awakening is always taken into full account and every course introduces unique elements.

All forms incorporate moving, sitting and standing postures that encourage the body to establish a true link to gravity in terms of the magnetism that can be applied. Each component of Lo Ban Pai offers a distinct contribution to the system as an integrated whole and can be combined in correspondence with other forms along a progressive path of learning.

INTERNAL MARTIAL ART

Embedded within the dynamic movement sets of Lo Ban Pai is a hidden martial art called Shadow Fist. Learning the warrior applications of the system is an advanced study and subject to invitation by Lujan. An extremely potent close-quarter system, Shadow Fist bears characteristics shared with numerous closely-guarded ancient combat arts and is highly adaptable. Wooden dummy is used as a training device in this evolved martial form. All external movements remain connected to the internal, their true source of power.

A QUANTUM PERSPECTIVE

Quantum science affirms the existence of an omnipresent shape of optimal motion in the known universe, commonly known as the Fibonacci sequence or the Golden ratio. Through the advent of this particular branch of physics this ancient knowledge has been substantiated in a way that satisfies the modern bias that requires a quantifiable measure of what was already perceivable.

All naturally occurring structures flow in these spirals at micro and macrocosmic levels, forming toroidal shapes like that of human and planetary energy fields.

Liquids, gasses and the growth patterns of organic and

inorganic forms all follow this adaptive format precisely for the reason that it allows energy to be applied most efficiently. Lo Ban Pai yields optimal results by following these same pathways.

The genius of how Lo Ban Pai cultivates electromagnetic potential is becoming apparent now that quantum science provides us with analogous insights and adequate syntax to describe what is actually taking place.

LINEAGE

The roots of Lo Ban Pai trace back to before the epoch of the Chinese Yellow Emperor (2500 BC). The pure forms and deeper applications of this exquisite art have been hidden until now. In the eighteenth century, master Lo Ban, a sea trader by profession, found his way to Mexico.

Upon settling there, he became involved with another ancient esoteric tradition known today as the Toltec path. He became the leader of that lineage and was henceforth known as the Nagual Lujan.

The only principle that he wished to absorb during his time in Mexico was the primary focus on the path with heart, and this remains the essential compass of Lo Ban Pai to this day. The master intuitive empath Lujan Matus is now the living embodiment of these transmitted teachings.

INTERWEAVING TIMELINES

The catalytic transmission Lujan received from Master Lo Ban, which manifested during a pivotal moment of his childhood at the age of seven, was subsequently revealed to have spanned many years of his current lifetime and, concurrently, several other alternate timelines. The intricacies of this time-bending initiation have been well documented in his first book, *The Art of Stalking Parallel Perception*, where a treasure-trove of key principles are introduced via this event and other defining encounters. In each edition that follows new elements are revealed, illuminating an odyssey that stretches one's perceptual bandwidth to encompass a non-linear paradigm.

By engaging in the discipline of Lo Ban Pai we begin to amalgamate past and future continuums within present consciousness. Since we don't live long enough to truly attain mastery in one lifetime, these practices allow one to access glimpses into alternate realities and provide the foundation to disseminate and ground that information into the precious moments that are continually escaping us.

To discover the secrets of our own personal journey reflects upon everyone's evolutionary status in the long run. One affects the whole and the whole affects one. Lo Ban Pai brings about fractalized experiences that are multiple, in comparison to one's situational consciousness being affected by only one reality.

When you contact this capacity, you can actualize the leaps that you need to achieve in this lifetime and not be subject to genetic memory loss and forget about what you have experienced and have to start all over again. These principles have been thoroughly elucidated in Lujan's fifth book, *Who Am I?*

When in contact with this consciousness, individuals

can act to affect their present timeline in a way that then subtly infuses the dynamic of their future, which is the true Mandela affect: to have consequences on past and present dynamics in terms of what one really realizes about what is meant to be applied in this lifetime.

Lujan has recovered five specific lifetimes, one of which revealed the memories that were contained within master Lo Ban's experiences. One of the gifts of Xoxonapo (also known as The Tenant, who is revealed in Lujan's first book) to master Lo Ban was the ability to reach his attention forward to become a new being and simultaneously retain the most pertinent memories from four previous lifetimes. These lifespans sustain master Lo Ban's power to reach a hand through the centuries to become Lujan Matus.

This principle applies equally to Lujan's current life experience. Four major lifetimes must be held in place through an act of power so he himself can reach forward five hundred years, which he has already achieved, to discover his next incarnation. This information has been documented in *Shadows in the Twilight.*

Within an altered state, in a deep parallel reality beyond the confines of this living construct, Lujan Matus received from master Lo Ban the entire scope of Lo Ban Pai.

As Lujan matures as a seer, the deeper aspects of perception, in terms of the full implications of master Lo Ban's transferal of consciousness, have far-reaching consequences that bring a deep state of reverence and humbleness to him in the present day.

The other continuums that Lujan has become aware of are as such mere glimpses. As his life unfolds he may reveal who he was and in turn the ramifications of these alternate memories will be applied in comparison to his living circumstances, to bear witness to that mystery that is continually unfolding in every instant.

One of the major forms that was transferred to Lujan Matus from master Lo Ban was the elegant movement sequence, known as *Dragon's Tears*. This set was created by him so as to help all practitioners of this art retain the subtle currents, the vibratory essence, the living frequency that one obtains when traversing bardo.

Dragon's Tears contains within it the ability to transform consciousness into an extremely profound trance-like state and includes static postures hidden within the movements that create astounding amounts of electric and magnetic power, as do all the forms of Lo Ban Pai.

WHO IS LUJAN MATUS?

Lujan Matus is a master intuitive empath with a unique ability to immerse individuals and groups in a rarefied state where the subtle currents of the interconnective universe become tangible. When *quantum entanglement* shifts from an abstract concept to a perceivable reality, we are automatically propelled into an entirely new way of being.

As a teacher and guide, Lujan is able to offer a genuine experience of how this actually *feels*. Once this is absorbed, anything that does not resonate with this quality of communion is innately understood to be void of meaning.

Lujan's comprehensive teachings provide lasting tools

to allow one to recognize and develop their own personal relationship with the unknown. As a person who has devoted himself to advanced physical, spiritual and interpersonal evolutionary principles and disciplines for a lifetime, his attainment as a human being is immediately evident. However, he does not beckon recognition for this but uses his capacities to invite exponential growth, in himself and in others, and this inner stance is revealed in his every gesture.

The unique transdimensional practices Lujan carries are priceless resource of wisdom and techniques that pertain directly to human evolution. His responsibility to embody and transmit that legacy defines his purpose and is the driving force behind his work.

Lujan Matus' initiation was set in motion at the age of seven when Master Lo Ban made his presence known in his life. Also known as the old nagual Lujan, this oriental seer imparted to him many treasures, including a variety of exceptionally powerful physical practices and deep awareness cultivation techniques that revolve absolutely around the adaptive axis of pure heart consciousness.

What this implies is not a rose-colored view that must be adopted in denial of what is manifesting in one's circumstance but a genuine engagement that takes into full account the profound cause and effect, responsibility and inextricable nature of each person's presence in this mysterious interdimensional continuum that envelops our consciousness.

THE WAY OF AN INTUITIVE EMPATH

Leaning towards the values of ancient Buddhism and esoteric Taoist teachings, Lujan embraces the all-encompassing view of empathy and compassion as the essential hallmarks of the philosophical basis of *Lo Ban Pai,* which is the name covering the full spectrum of his movement systems and meditative techniques. Lujan's teachings release shamanism from the subtexts latently embedded within a sorceric view, dethroning incongruent values in favor of the timeless wisdom that truly embodies the essence of the intelligence that arrives through emptiness. Journeying into this seemingly simple engagement, a seer begins to awaken to the highly sought-after ecstasy that abides within.

TEACHINGS, COURSES
AND ONLINE GUIDANCE

Within Lujan's online sessions and in the movement workshops he hosts around the world, a pervasive quality of profound empathy and spontaneity prevails. An implicit trust in following what arises in the moment as the greatest teacher available to us characterizes his approach at all times.

Decades of experience as a practitioner and teacher are brought to bear without applying preconceived methods in any given circumstance, for Lujan's deep commitment to ongoing evolution demands a total responsivity to the true flux of what is occurring. Through this non-dogmatic engagement, a rarefied space is created where eternity itself is beckoned to bear witness to what is unfolding. This quality of presence educates a receptive person to develop their own availability to the crucial insights and indications of the moment.

As an awakened intuitive empath Lujan devotes his full attention in service of the growth and liberation of every student in uncanny applications of momentary wisdom that embrace the totality of what is occurring within the group whilst simultaneously addressing individual issues and challenges that arise.

Thus, each teaching reveals genuine breakthroughs that foster an exponential growth that is utterly real and can neither be predetermined nor reproduced. Perhaps more than anything else, it is this atmosphere of acquiescence to the dictums of spirit that has the most profound impact on the lives of those who experience it firsthand. Many detailed personal testimonials written by students describing their experiences can be found at www.parallelperception.com.

PERSONAL POWER
THROUGH PHYSICAL MOVEMENT

The physical body is a resource uniquely tuned to act as a vehicle for the development of personal power: the very force that drives and guides one to embody a life of purpose and service. Lujan emphasizes the development and necessity of a clear connection to body awareness through regular practice, clean dietary choices and careful consideration of environmental factors.

The movement forms of Lo Ban Pai span a broad range of dynamic intensity, duration and have specific applications. Each sequence provides strong foundations for self-empowerment and all forms are absolutely complementary to one another.

What is so compelling about Lujan's courses are both the immediate physical results and their extraordinary effects on consciousness. Both as an intensely personal experience and within the remarkable metamorphoses of group consciousness, transformation occurs very quickly.

Observable effects become apparent as soon as one begins, for the system of Lo Ban Pai restores one's internal matrix to its true inherent power. The essential outcome revolves around the ability to realize that which is most valuable which appears right in front of you: A path with heart. In other words, to be attuned to a state of empathic communion.

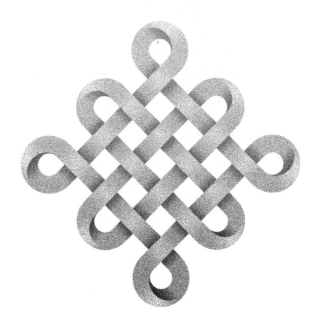

Lo Ban Pai

PROGRAM SUMMARY

TRAINING PROGRAMS

To enable students who attend in block weeks to learn in a traditional way, Lujan has developed standardized programs. This involves teaching certain details ahead of curriculum to lay a foundation that prepares students for future training while ensuring progression along a basic-to-advanced learning path. A wealth of personal testimonials that speak volumes about the direct benefits experienced by Lujan's students from all over the world can be found online. Please be invited to discover these profoundly inspiring accounts in the resources section of the Parallel Perception website.

Online Spiritual Guidance

ONLINE SPIRITUAL GUIDANCE

Online Spiritual Guidance is a program that takes place over a series of one-hour sessions and comprises special techniques, counseling and guidance for personal evolution.

Lujan's extraordinary ability to travel to the heart of the matter is as potent online as in person, and this program is an ideal introduction to his work, as well as a excellent alternative for those who are unable to travel to group courses and workshops. These one-on-one sessions follow a fluid format, adapting to the true needs of each individual's growth path.

Special techniques, such as The Eight Gates of Dreaming Awake and The Healing Meditation, are instrumental to this program, for they initiate a profound return to center: the essential starting point from which your journey of healing and transformation begins.

As a master intuitive empath, Lujan directly addresses what is most pertinent, without judgment, to support you to align with your life path. Tools and insights gained during this program empower ongoing growth, and upon completion you will be equipped to independently resolve any obstructions in your life. Your newfound sense of purpose will facilitate a complete and enduring transformation that will be able to be sustained following the conclusion of the sessions. This process will continue to deepen over time.

PROGRAM ELEMENTS INCLUDE:

- Instruction in the Eight Gates of Dreaming Awake
- Techniques to enhance inner silence
- Methods to develop intuitive empathy and precognitive abilities
- Meditations to promote physical healing
- How to enhance energy production during digestion
- Examining personal obstacles, barriers and challenges
- Revolutionary techniques for reclaiming your natural sovereign state
- Addressing issues surrounding one's personal application of heart consciousness
- Digital copies of all of Lujan's books are included as companion guides, with paperback copies available at an additional cost.

HEALING THE HEART

In all traditions where spirituality is an integral part of life, it is acknowledged that the center of our perception – and of our very being – is the heart.

This vital chakra is more than just the focal point of our emotions, or the organ that pumps blood and life force through our veins. It is the center from which we intuit, translate and process our experiences. Authentic guidance, therefore, must essentially begin with clearing our central matrix of all that blocks its free and natural expression.

Identifying the issues that surround a person's heart is the most direct way to embark upon a genuine spiritual journey. More often than not, these issues are related to what has been imprinted within a person's childhood and how these imprints have been – and often continue to be – prevalent in a person's life.

Whatever surrounds the heart creates an interpretation system that governs experience. More precisely, it impacts how you transform what occurs and how that defines you as an individual. A clear heart is synonymous with innocence, purity and courage.

To return to our original innocence, we have to be hone'st, vulnerable and raw. Initially, this can be a daunting prospect, for it may represent a loss of perceived 'advantage' or a frightening renouncement of the tactical behaviors developed over a lifetime. Even though we may continue to be injured by the perpetuation of defense mechanisms, strategies and fears that do not belong to the heart's realm, we are often afraid that giving them up will put us into a position of unbearable vulnerability.

However, when we arrive upon these pivotal realizations within a supportive environment, transformation becomes a viable alternative to perpetuation and newfound clarity gives power to the heart's quest to heal and evolve.

Overcoming Social Conditioning

During this course, you will have the opportunity to explore your unique circumstances to identify barriers to personal power and emotional freedom. This allows a permanent change of what one has become aware of. As Lujan accompanies you during these sessions he will assist you to process any upheavals that may arise so as to facilitate the growth of consciousness within a state of profound renewal.

These elements are in fact magical cues that have the potential to lead

us to a more awakened state, when interpreted from a spiritual perspective. From this point of acknowledgment we are re-acquainted with both the power and the responsibility we carry as co-creators of a living dream. Not only does this avail us to greater understanding of being subject to our expanded consciousness, it also unlocks our ability to transcend those behaviors, injuries and prejudices that created what has entrapped us.

INTUITIVE EMPATHY

True healing begins with a process of returning to innocence and rebuilding our strength from that foundation, which does not leave room for unwholesome elements or manipulative tools. In spirituality, as in life, what we want is not always what we need and a predetermined format may not be the most beneficial path to follow.

This is why online guidance with Lujan Matus, who is recognized as a master intuitive empath, is directed by clear and unmistakable indications of the moment. Thus what is applied within these sessions is in accordance with the true dictums of your heart path in order to enable maximum growth and learning.

For some this may seem to be mysterious as a format but those who participate testify that this approach produces unprecedented personal revelations and deep energetic transformation.

TECHNIQUES FOR
TRANSFORMATION AND GROWTH

All of Lujan's techniques are clearly defined, tangibly effective, and can immediately be applied whether one has previous experience with this kind of work or not. The profoundly meditative state that results from this application will bring about a laser-like clarity to your perception that is all-encompassing. This will in turn progressively open consciousness to one's personal source of inspiration, which informs and serves to guide you about needs, issues, and crucial directives pertinent to fully embracing your true potential.

These practices will also yield other remarkable results. One such primary outcome is a feeling of extreme comfort that develops whereby the body does not want to leave its newfound sanctuary of unadulterated silence, which is a powerful motivator for ongoing commitment to personal growth. Déjà vu and precognition are amongst the other unique types of seeing that will begin to emerge.

THE EIGHT GATES OF DREAMING AWAKE

Passing through these eight internal thresholds, guided by the steady instruction of Lujan's voice, you will find yourself entering into a most exquisite state of inner silence. This uniquely effective technique, known as the Eight Gates of Dreaming Awake, allows one to directly access the ever-present quietude at the center of one's being. Upon your rediscovery of this internal sanctuary, a profound trance-like inducement allows Lujan to guide you beyond any socialized barriers that may appear.

With practice the warrior begins to experience long periods of inner silence until it becomes second nature. As you become clearer, you will be able to view your life from a renewed perspective and determine fresh approaches to familiar circumstances. Previously unseen solutions naturally present themselves and new neural pathways are formed, supporting your continuous evolution upon a path of heart.

Return to Body Consciousness

Lujan will instruct you how to dive deeply into the center of your photonic potential and become grounded within the central matrix of your body consciousness. The practice will not only affect the practitioner but also anybody in their immediate vicinity, propelling them into inner silence and a feeling of exquisite comfort.

Using a remarkably simple method, Lujan will show you how to redirect your eyes, ears and breath to the appropriate directions in order to reclaim an original state of pure being.

This arrival allows a permanent change of what one has become aware of and cultivates an enduring connection with our original nature. The practical applications of these techniques, based upon the principles of Being, Knowing And Not-Doing, are outlined in detail in the workbook manual *Whisperings of the Dragon: Shamanic Practices to Awaken Your Primal Power*, which Lujan specifically wrote as a guideline for this course. His latest publication, *Who Am I*, is also provided to more deeply elucidate the subtler aspects of empathic communion.

HEALING MEDITATION

The Healing Meditation is an ancient technique to connect the hands with the lower cauldron. This practice facilitates enormous amounts of bioelectromagnetic energy to stream through the body, which allows you to view your own luminous cocoon from within and direct your chi for healing.

You will simultaneously learn a method to generate and circulate the energy from food around the body so as to allow the body to become physically stronger.

The effect of this meditative system is that it changes the bioelectromagnetic field to accommodate quantum shifts for the individual practitioner. Additionally, it will inadvertently restructure the fundamental fabric of one's environment via universal principles of modulation and resonance.

In essence, recalibration of the elements derived from the quantum reality will adapt in true correspondence to the directives of the command issued by the consciousness at the time of arrival within any given moment.

5 online sessions

LO BAN PAI

INITIATION SERIES

The initiation series builds a foundation for Oriental shamanism by preparing the body, will and energy system. It teaches movement structures, physical training methods and chi cultivation that is applied specifically to energy awakening, healing and balancing.

GRAVITY

GRAVITY

Gravity is a very beautiful, simple system of elegant movements that aligns the practitioner with the six directions, introduces the harmonies and establishes the foundation for the luminous cocoon as an energy bubble to be tangibly realized.

It is an indoor practice deeply grounded within the innermost structure of Lo Ban Pai that activates the capacity for the practitioner to connect with the inner workings of the fascia via internal alignments that are applied within every other form. Though Gravity contains advanced teachings, it is essential that it be implemented at the very beginning since it establishes crucial principles for all following programs.

INTRODUCTION TO THE SIX DIRECTIONS AND THE TWO HARMONIES

Being instructed in the Gravity series informs your biofield how to focus your energy within the six directions and contains detailed teachings in the application of the harmonies.

In the beginning of this program you will learn how to focus your intention in a forward, linear fashion, which, in combination with further techniques that are revealed in this form, develops your capacity to internally activate your radiance.

Gravity practices inevitably expand the voluminous viscosity of the energy bubble, 360-degrees and in the six directions, which will continue to increase in both scope and density as one matures in this discipline.

PHOTONS AND THE EXPANSION OF RADIANCE

Regularly performing the Gravity series will allow you to obtain the intentions within another's body when you are in proximity with them, as long as your intent is pure. It will also develop your capacity to intuitively know when another human being's awareness is focused upon your luminous bubble, even from great distances. These abilities are contingent upon an empty perspective on your part, one that bears no agenda.

In tandem with the physical gestures, you will learn methods of sending your etheric roots deep into the ground and simultaneously drawing energy from the sky into the body. Practitioners report powerful sensations during these exercises that confirm reciprocity from the environment.

One's field of potential becomes so voluminous that this practice eventually yields access to the matrix that is the blueprint of the planet.

Elements that bear relevance to your circumstance are naturally revealed as you absorb chi from the environment. In other words, information about what is currently active in that vast auric field spontaneously becomes available to your awareness.

Some have referred to this kind of phenomena as

accessing the Akashic files, which is most often interpreted as a kind of cosmic vault of past and future records. This framework within itself opens up the contradictory terms of time being identified in a linear format. However, our actual experience also encompasses non-linear processes, within the profound mysteries of our circumstance revealing itself in the ever-present moment that is continually escaping us.

HEALTH AND MAGNETISM

Gravity increases the practitioner's ability to absorb and store the appropriate light photons, which the body innately knows to draw towards itself. It will always take exactly what is needed and nothing more, if that particular frequency is available in the surrounding environment.

Amongst the treasures belonging to the Gravity series is a rare technique that teaches you how to use the lower dantien to increase the capacity of the body to send chi into the four extremities through a method of compression that allows one to collect and store energy.

Essential breathing techniques are introduced that

deepen your connection to the practice and educate one to the subtle yet crucial difference that refined breath work makes to movement, presence and perception.

HARVESTING ELECTROMAGNETIC CHI

Through profound grounding and bone alignment techniques, combined with specific visualizations, Gravity opens up internal spiral pathways within the biofield to facilitate an unimpeded flow of electric and magnetic chi.

No previous training or experience is required to engage in this form, and profound outcomes will be observable from the beginning. Extraordinary collective results have been experienced during Gravity workshops, whereby entire groups are simultaneously affected by pronounced electromagnetic phenomena.

CONNECTIVITY AND LO BAN PAI

Though a standalone practice within itself, the principles of Gravity fortify every other form. Through applying what is learned in this primary series your gestures will become infused with tangible vitality, which directly allows one to realize the importance of this finely tuned connection to our electric and magnetic potential, both in Lo Ban Pai and in life.

5 Day Program

OPENING THE TAO

Opening the Tao

This is a powerful movement set that enhances every aspect of Lo Ban Pai. Though introduced by Lujan to the public only recently, Opening the Tao and Gravity are the mother forms, where all possibilities are birthed. These sequences give novices the immediate experience of the inherent power within their electromagnetic potential, which becomes available as voluminous magnetism felt within the hands and periphery of the body. Specific effects on the human bio-electromagnetic field become apparent through its orbits, which charge the DNA and initiate an irreversible catalyst toward transdimensional consciousness.

DOORWAY TO
YOUR LIVING DREAM

Opening the Tao is a comprehensive movement system that ushers in a profound renewal of your relationship with the world around you.

We are always at a point of reception and we are always on a threshold of discovery. There's no position that can govern our awareness other than where we are at now. Our journey determines us and who we are is revealed to us at every moment.

The beauty of this foundation form is that it truly sows the seeds for developing an alternate cognitive system, which is not a reasonable faculty but a perceptual process that allows you to discover exactly what's in front of you via your awakened body consciousness.

ROOTS, ROTATIONAL AXES
AND THE TOROIDAL FIELD

The movements of Opening the Tao, in combination

with special breathing techniques, generate an intense magnetism that surrounds the body, while the orbits following each set enable gathering and sealing that electromagnetic energy within one's central matrix, thus charging the toroidal field.

Our physicality is stabilized by our lower limbs, which can be likened to the roots of a tree. Beginning with powerful grounding sequences, Opening the Tao strengthens the bones, fortifies tendons and ligaments, and increases muscular stamina, thoroughly revitalizing one's structural integrity.

Practicing this powerful sequence will solicit an immediate response from your core and you will begin to realize there are vortices of energy surrounding your physical form that are being nourished and circulated by every gesture. The implications of this particular phenomenon, though initially most evident in terms of developing one's body consciousness, extend far beyond the material plane.

LIVING ALCHEMY

The interconnectivity of our entire universe is based upon luminous exchange, and collecting light is something everybody does all the time, whether the mind is aware of it or not. It is our body that recognizes the frequencies that arrive.

Refining our ability to absorb and fluidly interpret photonic information is an art at the cutting edge of the evolution of humankind. Though not currently widely acknowledged by the general populous, this revelatory information about the extensive influence of photons upon consciousness is beginning to surface.

The human biofield remains one of the most sophisticated of all interfaces. Recognizing and becoming responsive to the intricacies of luminous communion is an integral aspect of Lo Ban Pai. Many of the key methods to cultivate one's receptivity to this continuous exchange are introduced within the Initiate Series.

HEALTH BENEFITS

Opening the Tao initiates a profound cleanse from the inside out, reactivating one's lymphatic system and eliminating acidity from muscles, sinuses and lungs. Bone density is also steadily increased via these movements, thus sustaining the integrity of one's skeletal structure further into the aging process.

The forms rotational gestures cause the synovial fluid to be evenly distributed throughout the joints. This sacred liquid is then transformed by the frequency obtained through diligent practice, which influences the light photons to generate radiance via the consciousness of the practitioner.

ENERGETIC EVOLUTION

This unique series of exercises creates a vacuum joining the physical and energy body through specific elliptical orbits. This is how one can gain access to higher frequencies and actually see the light generated by the body. As realizations amass within through sustained practice, emptiness gathers. In

Tibetan culture this is known as being 'Hollow Boned', which refers to a deeply silent awareness.

Opening up the rotational axes of every joint initiates a catalytic process towards new levels of receptivity to the universe at large. The early forms of Lo Ban Pai provide a visceral introduction to this fascinating premise, which is explored in greater depths in the Intermediate and Advanced series'.

Optimal practice time: early morning.

5 Day Program

Awakening the Energy Body

AWAKENING THE ENERGY BODY

Awakening the Energy Body is one of four initiation practices towards establishing the magnetic, directional capacities of the practitioner.

This program teaches dynamic exercises that open the meridian channels and encourage energy to stream through them. It contains Thunder Dance, Palm Activation training and the rarely taught Fire Turtles chi gong sequence. This form opens up the central channel, from the mid-spine to the sacrum, lengthening from the middle of the scapula to the base of the skull and activating synovial fluids between the joints. Strengthens muscular and tendon systems and creates quiet, sustainable fortitude.

ACTIVATION OF SPIRAL PATHWAYS

Awakening the Energy Body is one of four primary entry programs to the Dragon system that Lujan teaches throughout Lo ban Pai. Within this form he imparts the fundamental movements that promote energy cultivation through the principles of Spiral Energetics to awaken the body and enliven the internal energy channels.

In this sequence the initiate acquires various methods to clear physical and energetic blockages in order to cultivate optimal flow of chi, which inevitably nurtures the vascular, limbic and parasympathetic systems.

DRAGON GATES

Entering Dragon Gates is the key to experiential spiritual growth in Lo Ban Pai. These etheric portals are elusive, yet ever-present and right in front of us; within us and all around us at all times. They are called the gates of the dragon via the fact that one feels them yet they cannot be seen. When the initiate passes through such a threshold the experience is never left behind, perennially persisting until fully integrated within.

Activate Body Consciousness

For energy cultivation to be successful, the body must be switched on so as to become aware and receptive to the elusive dynamics that are all-encompassing and surrounding us at every moment. As the name implies, Awakening the Energy Body contains many potent sequences that directly address this fundamental necessity.

Conditioning for Alignment

In Awakening the Energy Body you will be taught how to lengthen and activate ligaments and tendons so as to realign your being with the primordial essence of your power. While some elements are physically demanding, the disciplined practitioner will be greatly rewarded with a significant increase in physical fitness, strength and endurance, as well as mental clarity and focus.

This form greatly increases stamina and willpower,

enabling the practitioner to harness their unbending intent in order to facilitate transformation.

ENERGY CULTIVATION: FIRE TURTLES AND PEARL-POPPING

Within Awakening the Energy Body Lujan will instruct you in the rarely taught Fire Turtles chi gong and Whip-snake sequence. Including these powerful sets within one's practice generates explosive chi and encourages it to stream throughout the body's entire field via a pounding pressure that emanates from the heart center, enlivening and opening energetic channels both internally and externally.

Pearl-popping is a method to allow the individual to flip their dantien backwards and forwards within the body. This teaches one to maneuver this vital center in a relaxed manner.

You will also be introduced to Walking the Tao, a subtle energy-circulating sequence that initiates expansion of the toroidal field of the heart, which in turn strengthens the magnetism of the hands.

Introducing Spiral Energetics

Learning how to coil via the golden equation through movement is the basic essence of Lo Ban Pai. Also called Spiral Energetics, this is Oriental shamanism that reveals the essence of the Tao. The system employs coiling gestures to access, activate, nurture and apply energy. Lo Ban Pai centers around heart consciousness and all movement employed within every form supports this.

Program Elements Included in Awakening the Energy Body

Instruction in a self-massage technique that enlivens the external 'wei chi', which is our protective immunity that emanates from the skin. This easy-to-apply personal care routine slows down the aging process.

The Thunder Dance: A dynamic rhythmic sequence that employs a trance rhythm, this is a powerful space-clearing practice that can be used anywhere.

Depending on the aptitude of the student, portions of the following program – Windlock – will be introduced as preparation for the next step.

5 Day Program

WINDLOCK SYSTEM

THE WINDLOCK SYSTEM

The Windlock system is a physical regimen that literally reshapes the body inside and out, stimulating energy flow whilst awakening the chakras and internal organs through specific, targeted shock motions that bi-directionally activate the inguinal crease (known as the Qua) in combination with the shoulder nest.

This program provides the essential elements often neglected or concealed in most energy cultivation disciplines and expands upon dragon coiling techniques introduced in Opening the Tao. One of the most magnetic and electric of the initiation forms, Windlock is dynamic within its application and develops fortitude and directness.

PACKING CHI

The Windlock system is an invigorating practice that balances energy channels and reshapes the body. Its dynamic movements are performed in static postures while specific breathing is applied. This form solicits rapid physical transformation and raises one's optimism.

ENERGY AND BODY CONSCIOUSNESS

Lujan emphasizes the importance of the physical body as an integral part of spiritual development. Windlock activates the bioelectromagnetic field in specific ways to prepare it as a vehicle for the warrior to cultivate energy for enhanced awareness. At a fundamental level it elevates the practitioner's body consciousness as their primary vehicle for transformation.

TRANSFORMATIONAL RESULTS

Windlock is extremely rejuvenating and fortifies immunity through cleansing the lymphatic system and reverses one's biological clock. After practicing this athletic form for six months, your body will return to a late teens/early twenties physique. Optimal results are obtained by adopting a specific dietary regime that supports this process.

(See Raw Food Solution for detailed information on complementary nutritional options).

The Windlock system helps unite one's inner core within a central energetic matrix that runs from the perineum to the crown. It tightens and binds the muscles to the bones, causing the warrior to have an extremely lean and muscular appearance.

CULTIVATION OF AN ENERGETIC FRAMEWORK

Windlock develops an abstract container around the body: a defined framework in space. This energetic perimeter sets up internal reference points inside the container that alerts the warrior to their internal power. This includes knowing where optimal movements start and stop, which in turn develops the recoil response applied in the advanced practice of Shadow Fist Kung Fu.

Windlock movements give linear shocks to the limbs that send energy in spirals through the body. These waves activate specific chakras determined by which movement is performed. The practice simultaneously opens and clears the meridian system to create an unimpeded bio-electromagnetic flow of chi, but maintains it within the integral perimeter, a sealed space.

A SHAMAN'S VIEWPOINT

Windlock is the empath's guide to power and enables the warrior to embody the essence of the Taoist way. Through these movements, joy and happiness will be in abundance by virtue of one's youth returning. The contained energetic framework cultivated through Windlock will also support your internal resilience via the magnetism obtained through persistent practice.

MARTIAL ARTS

The Windlock System supplies the warrior with the

fundamentals of Shadow Fist Kung Fu. No matter which style one practices, it is imperative to integrate the Windlock techniques to establish the power necessary to be effective whilst remaining as stable as an oak tree and as flexible as bamboo.

At the end of this program Lujan will also introduce Shadow Fist applications that increase one's personal power and build confidence.

It is not required to be a kung fu practitioner to succeed in this program. It is only necessary to apply oneself to the principles of what one is learning. In essence the word 'kung fu' means to develop personal integrity through the act of devoting oneself to a practice.

IN THE WINDLOCK PROGRAM
YOU WILL LEARN:

- Binding core muscles to the central matrix

- Age-reversal techniques

- Locking movements

- Opening, clearing and balancing of energy meridians

- Toning of internal organs, reinvigorate chakras

- Increasing the perimeter of the energy bubble

- Harmonization of left and right hemispheres via increasing one's neuroplasticity

  Optimal practice time: early morning.

  5 Day Program

LO BAN PAI
INTERMEDIATE SERIES

The intermediate series applies cultivated energy in trance-inducing movement and dynamic forms designed to channel chi and awareness for spiritual development by actively connecting with the principles of heaven and earth, which combine with the essence of man. The practitioner learns to direct internal chi in pragmatic and ever-evolving formats.

www.parallelperception.com

GOLDEN LOTUS

GOLDEN LOTUS

The Golden Lotus series cultivates chi to stream through and restore balance to the physical and energy body. It functions similarly to 'medical' or 'longevity' chi gong, by absorbing and storing the mysterious luminescence that emanates from the full moon (known in Sanskrit as Soma). Applied in combination with the elemental meditation technique that is illustrated in the book Awakening the Third Eye, this graceful set enlivens the capacity to become lucidly focused within one's dreams. Advanced dragon coiling is introduced in this sequence.

SEAMLESS INTEGRATION OF TWO FORMS

This program teaches two sets that are seamlessly woven together as one. The Quetzalcoatl is the shorter sequence with a specific healing focus, which was originally called The Mayan Winged Serpent Series and was taught by Quetzalcoatl in Central America, 1500 years ago. This was integrated into the original Golden Lotus to create an advanced form that has a wider energy cultivation scope and higher potency as a health and longevity practice, with an added element of healing through the absorption of Soma (the nurturing frequency of the moon).

The series contains wide sweeping circles that trace lines all around the body to create a vibrant matrix in the energy field.

This blueprint is nourished and strengthened with daily morning practice performed indoors.

Golden Lotus is a medical chi gong regimen that equals the most powerful practices found in the Orient. This form builds a functional bridge between personal life force and universal energy and gives access to the ability to store chi in the dantiens. It is the beginning of the Intermediate level of Lo Ban Pai.

THE HEALING ENERGY OF THE MOON

Once a month the Golden Lotus is performed in front of the full moon. Moon energy has a special healing quality. This beautiful form is a unique way to cultivate the skill of connecting to vibrational fields at large.

This set is practiced in a static stance that builds strength and endurance. This establishes within the practitioner a wellspring of electric and magnetic potential that is absorbed from the moon and rises up through the body to the palms to inadvertently embrace the sky through devotional gestures.

ENERGY CULTIVATION

Golden Lotus is the first major energy cultivation set. Together with the Fire Turtles and the initial Twisted Root techniques learned in the Gravity series, it helps ground the very important element of storing chi within the practitioner's discipline.

This form beckons the force of the infinite to make itself felt, thus learning to sense and connect with electromagnetism at large which also has applications for the development of awareness.

HEALTH AND LONGEVITY CHI GONG.

The ancient Oriental approach to health is systemic and holistic. This translates into medical chi gong, also known as a devotional practice, that works to balance and unblock on one hand, while strengthening and nurturing simultaneously.

Diseased aspects of the biofield are aligned towards harmony while healthy elements are supported to establish sustainability and longevity. A healthy system is each warrior's unique and custom-built tool for transformation.

Moon Gazing Techniques

The Golden Lotus has an accompanying elemental gazing technique – described in Lujan's book Awakening the Third Eye – where the practitioner absorbs the moon's energy and utilizes its caress for healing. These profoundly trance-inducing meditations are practiced after performing the set when the moon is full.

Lucid Dreaming

The Golden Lotus is used for inducing very deep states of lucidity. Unlike normal dreaming, practicing this form produces visionary imagery that contains an enormous amount of information.

This series awakens the dreamer with plasmic shocks to the lower dantien that simultaneously impact the third eye and result in seeing a white light, which are the filaments produced by the elixir 'Soma'. The reality of becoming fully aware within one's dreams whilst being subject to a trance-induced state between sleeping and waking becomes available.

This occurs via the fact that the energy of the full moon imprints upon the consciousness of the practitioner, thus opening a visionary portal instead of the dreamer falling into imprinted socialized sequences.

The practice is repeated four times evenly spaced during the night of the full moon. This produces a very unique lucidity in combination with the Ascension moon-gazing techniques elucidated in Awakening the Third Eye.

INTERNAL REALIZATIONS

The practice of the Golden Lotus is trained on a daily basis so as to fortify the physical neural net in terms of becoming familiar with electromagnetic possibilities that are inherently embedded within the movements.

The initiate will learn to reconnect with their sovereign central matrix and to take present composites of data to be resolved in conjunction with all the techniques that are introduced in Awakening the Third Eye.

5 Day Program

DRAGON'S TEARS

www.parallelperception.com

Dragon's Tears

Dragon's Tears is the most trance-inducing of all the forms in Lo Ban Pai, which will prompt the practitioner to be guided by heart awareness to awaken the self within the highest vibrational frequency. This unique form is the master key to those who seek their freedom within the truth of their heart-path, for it will ultimately equip the seer to move forward with integrity and power within their life. This elegant sequence initiates the empty force as a powerful ally. Within this set are hidden static standing postures that develop the essence of Ling Kong Jing, which is the purest reflection of the ancient Tao that is initiated in connection to void consciousness.

This elegant energy cultivation form reveals to the warrior the transcendent essence of our true nature. It is a timeless form that flows like water, generating powerful and soothing chi, which courses in and around the body.

The Tears of the Dragon introduce the initiate to the Indigo spectrum of light; the highest form of frequency that beckons us to be aware of it at all times.

Disciplined practice of Dragon's Tears will dramatically impact your life, clearing stagnant energy and strengthening the body as well as enhancing perception, health and longevity.

Awakening Body Consciousness

Dragon's Tears helps one forget themselves – the socially embedded being – so that one can remember the most precious gift we have; the intangible self that witnesses its own journey at the moment that escapes our ability to possess it.

The primary impact that this has on human awareness is to subdue the internal social underpinnings so that one's body consciousness may be awakened absolutely.

The energetic waves that gently pulsate through one's being dissolve all manner of machinations until one is free to experience the beauty of oneself, thus expanding into the magnificence of heartfelt unity with all that is.

ENERGY ACTIVATION

The energy accessed when practicing Dragon's Tears is immediately tangible, by virtue of the fact that it activates each chakra individually. The effects may be perceived as an intense electromagnetism in the hands, which eventually saturates one's whole being, or as subtle circulating energetic currents that caress the skin as they are gently absorbed.

TRANSFORMATION OF AWARENESS

The introduction of these exercises immediately transforms awareness through a physicality that awakens dormant aspects of perception. From the outset, one is brought into a state of heightened consciousness that comes about through the stimulation of both physical and energetic channels in the body and the absorption of one's attention in this magical practice.

UNIQUE MOVEMENTS AKIN TO CHI GONG

Visually the form bears some resemblance to ancient Chinese Chi Gong, yet has its own unique fluidity, immediacy and subtle power that distinguish its character and results. Its circular sweeping movements address the full sphere of the energy body, following invisible magnetic currents that increasingly come to the forefront of awareness for the practitioner.

Once the warrior reaches a level of competency, the body appears to be rotating on many axes at once, while the directional path of each gesture remains clear and unbroken as one's attention becomes unified with the movements.

Lucid Dreaming: Group Consciousness

When practicing the Dragon's Tears, one of the most noted effects that occurs in large workshops – other than the trance-like state it promotes – is that many participants align and begin to dream lucidly with Lujan.

When learning this series, deep delta to epsilon brainwave patterns are reached. This allows the initiate to become aware of the corresponding pattern that creates lucid dreaming. Here is where Lujan will retrieve you and teach you

Dragon's Tears in a visionary state during your sleeping hours.

This is a two-week program consisting of two levels that can be undertaken as single weeks if preferred. This provides the student with the opportunity to learn the program in two separate 5-day sessions or attend for the complete two-week program.

Level 1: 5 Days
Level 2: 5 Days
Complete Program: 10 Days

WHISPERING PALMS

WHISPERING PALMS

Whispering Palms is a signature form that transmits the fundamental esoteric keys for the entire movement family of Lo Ban Pai. It is a very deep energy cultivation practice and establishes a strong foundation for martial forms. This program instructs the practitioner in their integration of meditative awareness, which opens up the electromagnetic force to rise through the physical form and be utilized. It awakens the mysterious essence of one's internal power

VOID ESSENCE

Whispering Palms is a comprehensive energy cultivation form that utilizes rotational postures, which stabilize the central force through the alignment of the energy centers: the lower, middle and upper dantiens.

The mystery of Lo Ban Pai becomes increasingly palpable as a conscious kinesthetic experience via the movements. This powerful sequence enhances perception of the magnetism that emanates from the hands, which in turn boosts the capacity to collect and store chi.

This heightened awareness of electromagnetic connectivity promotes the ability to align with a deep reservoir of sincerity within the self, which fosters the elusive state of communion with spirit.

THE TIBETANS, TWISTED ROOTS, EMPERORS AND CONTINUAL KNOT SEQUENCES

Whispering Palms is a beautiful, elegantly woven series of fluid coiling movements that trace energy pathways in and around the body. It comprises a succession of forms arranged in four sets: The Tibetans, Twisted Roots, Emperors and Continual Knot sequence, which can be practiced independently of one another. An optional 'Gateway' set can be inserted between each of these modules to strengthen the magnetic potential being drawn from the earth via the legs.

The practitioner can adapt the series in accordance with their own physical fitness levels. This allows the roots of one's being to systematically develop the power necessary for the most demanding application of the set.

CHI CULTIVATION AND INTERNAL ALCHEMY

Whispering Palms cultivates a very potent and dense electromagnetic field through the principles of Spiral Energetics. Having enlivened, absorbed and stored that energy the practitioner retains a photonic awareness of that potential throughout their day. This awareness alerts the student to the full spectrum of influences within their environment, which enhances intuitive receptivity.

Chi cultivation is also improved by establishing a tangible bridge between the lao-gung points on the palms, and the lower dantien. This is required to become aware of the full spectrum of internal alchemy that is being activated via this sequence. This pulsating connectivity allows the student to be both a practitioner of internal work (neijia) and to have a point of reference to self-adjust movements through direct biofeedback.

Traditionally this technique is taught by an unnecessarily long and arduous approach. Lujan supersedes this method by applying direct transmission through expanding his electromagnetic field while in the presence of the student. This allows the initiate to become acutely aware of their potential for future development through direct experience.

ESOTERIC SECRETS OF THE DRAGON GATES

Whispering Palms provides a vehicle for daily interaction with, and a sensory-based experience of, what Lujan calls 'eternity'; that ineffable mystery beyond the confines of our socialized awareness.

Energy cultivation creates a platform for esoteric practices and Whispering Palms brings both these together by engaging the Dragon Gates. These natural electromagnetic vortexes emanate from the body and into the energy field at specific locations.

Dragon gates are sealed by socialization and this practice opens, nurtures and activates them so their true functionality is restored, as two-way portals between self and eternity.

This requires the application of the secret essence of the Tao, such as sincere action, and the use of movements known as 'shen-gongs', which align one with the true potential of the human spirit, personally and collectively.

Learning what it means and how to enter a Dragon Gate is the spiritual gift of this program and the source of the name Whispering Palms. With this skill the warrior can beckon eternity, and eternity can respond in harmonic resonance to manifest what can be described as a most intimate and transformational communion with the ineffable void itself.

Oriental Shamanism and Modern Science

Lujan describes the spiral energetic principles of Lo Ban Pai in terms of Quantum mechanics. This marriage between ancient oriental shamanism and modern science is a novel way to contextualize what actually occurs as palpable phenomena instead of mere theory. The function and application of energy vortexes, Fibonacci spirals and the bridging of time-space with Dragon Gates becomes available as a real experience with profound implications for personal growth.

INTERNAL MARTIAL ARTS

If the student is capable, the preliminary 'half-moon step' is introduced, preparing the practitioner for Temple Bagua: one of the most advanced practices. This stepping can be incorporated with the last part of Whispering Palms, thereby adding a walking element. If the student is not ready to absorb this information, this movement will be taught in the Binding Roots program.

HEALING MEDITATION

Lujan teaches the Healing Meditation in conjunction with Whispering Palms. This technique has been a closely guarded secret for centuries. It facilitates the connection of the palms to the lower dantien, which allows the individual to become connected to the true source of their internal alchemy.

Whispering Palms program includes:

- Connect the palms to the lower dantien, the earth and the sky
- Generate and store energy
- Sense, open and activate your Dragon Gates
- Follow energy to optimize chi cultivation
- Develop self-correction through biofeedback
- The art of sincerity
- Healing meditation

5 Day Program

The Three Treasures

THE THREE TREASURES

This powerful set cultivates the three treasures of Jing, Chi and Shen, and is the essential foundation for all further intermediate practices within Lo Ban Pai.

It is both a stand-alone energy cultivation form and progressively integrates the two following movement sets of the intermediate series: Jaguar and Small Mountain.

CULTIVATION OF THE SACRED TRINITY

The Three Treasures of Jing, Chi and Shen is a familiar concept in Eastern energetic arts and internal alchemy. Although there are no exact translations for these terms they are generally interpreted as Essence, Energy and Spirit.

Each element is important on its own, but in combination, they are the key to utilizing one's life force to enhance holistic equilibrium and develop a harmonized body consciousness.

The essential goal of all Oriental healing arts is to cultivate, balance and expand the Three Treasures. Jing is transformed into Chi and then into Shen and in this process, we nourish the spirit.

The Three Treasures set, as taught by Lujan Matus, combines focused chi cultivation with advanced dragon coiling as its essential core. It is a multi-level practice, complete in itself, and is also designed to include two additional sets that are added in as they are learned.

THE THREE VITAL ENERGY CONTAINERS

The Three Treasures are known as: Jing—our essence, the primordial energy we inherit from our parents and that we are born with; Chi—our vital force, the energy that flows in and around our bodies and keeps us alive; and Shen—our spirit, our sacred self.

Internal alchemy practices for transmuting these energies are traditionally referred to as "refining essence (Jing) into breath (Chi), refining breath (Chi) into spirit (Shen), and refining spirit (Shen) and returning to Emptiness."

The three major cauldrons in the body where energy resides are the lower, middle and upper dantiens. Each of these must be constantly activated and replenished so as to generate vibrant health and clarity of perception.

Whereas Jing is stored in the lower dantien; Chi circulates throughout the body, and is also housed in the lower dantien, Shen resides within the heart in combination with the third eye and radiates outward from the whole body. This is why people who have cultivated strong Shen seem to be surrounded by auras of light. The light of someone's Shen is also said to shine brightly through their eyes.

Dragon coiling acts as a catalyst to activate and open the dantiens to prepare them for absorption of Jing, Chi and Shen. They become stabilized through the creation of a symbiotic connection between one's awareness and the voluminous potential of these three activated vortexes.

JING: ESSENTIAL ENERGY

The Jing essence is stored in the lower cauldron, which is located slightly below the navel region within the center of the body. This is the primordial essence that we are born with. In order to sustain health, Jing must be constantly nourished by Shen and Chi.

Jing is the source of all development and growth in the body and spirit, and it is closely associated with the sexual energy that forms the basis of our body's essential life force.

It nourishes our entire organism, especially the reproductive system. It is Jing that imbues every aspect of our lives with the potentiality for development from birth until death, from conception to accomplishment.

CHI: BODY CONSCIOUSNESS

The second cauldron is located in the area of the heart chakra and is the primary vortex where Chi gathers. The essence of Jing and Shen are mixed in this central vortex to be transformed and redistributed throughout the other centers. This in turn, strengthens the whole body consciousness.

Many translate Chi as energy, or life force. In the body, it is closely associated with the respiratory system and the breath (like 'Prana'). In many ways, every metabolic process, every movement, every emotion, every thought, every flickering of consciousness is both governed by, and a direct manifestation of, one's Chi.

SHEN: INTERDIMENSIONAL AWARENESS

Shen is created through the harmonious union of Jing and Chi, which gives birth to the true self as an entirely new being. Shen shows us our own experiences and guides us through transformation, both inner and outer. It allows us to

107

see and experience parallel realities.

When the heart center is clear and abundant the upper cauldron of the third eye – where the Shen essence resides – becomes activated, connecting the practitioner to multidimensional aspects of their perception

KUNG FU ALCHEMY
AND ORIENTAL SHAMANISM

Not only does the Three Treasures infuse the martial forms with electromagnetism but all of the other sequences within Lo Ban Pai also feed the practice of the Three Treasures. This is possible mainly because the martial forms follow lines of motion determined by the flow of various energies in the body and the expanded biofield surrounding it.

The martial sets incorporated into the Three Treasures are: 1. The Jaguar Series

2. The Small Mountain Series

Once both Jaguar and Small Mountain have been learned they complete the Three Treasures form as one whole.

HOLISTIC PRACTICE

Performing the martial sets is in fact akin to Chi Gong and Nei Gong, for they also follow the Fibonacci principle of spiraling, which in Lo Ban Pai is called dragon coiling.

In contrast to most martial arts, where energy is developed in one practice (chi gong) so that it may be applied in other sets, Lo Ban Pai training saves time with no loss of effectiveness by consistently adopting a comprehensive approach whereby every form progressively addresses many layers of development simultaneously.

The primary focus of the Three Treasures set specifically cultivates the awareness of Jing, Chi and Shen within one form. There is no segregation where these vital elements are developed individually. Again, this supports the amalgamation of the three essential energies as they appear in 'real life', coexisting simultaneously.

INTERNAL MARTIAL ARTS

If the student is capable, the preliminary 'half-moon step' is introduced, preparing the practitioner for Temple Bagua: one of the most advanced practices. This stepping can be incorporated with the last part of Whispering Palms, thereby adding a walking element. If the student is not ready to absorb this information, this movement will be taught in the Binding Roots program.

DNA ACTIVATION

The ancient Chinese approach to spiritual development does not emphasize theoretical concepts. Instead, practical techniques are employed to foster esoteric insight as a primary goal while nurturing the energies required to realize the uniqueness of one's own path.

The Three Treasures set allows the practitioner to activate the dormant capacity of DNA to reawaken and heal the body from within. This opens vast new horizons to be explored.

While we practice the Three Treasures, a portion of our energetic structure phases out of this dimension momentarily. In doing so it accumulates information from other realities that is brought back as knowledge that is pertinent to the practitioner's evolution. This insight can be utilized and realized if our essential three treasures are clear and open.

The Three Treasures are immensely useful for anyone, especially those interested in Primordial Shen Gong, which becomes available as an option upon completion of the Intermediate Series.

5 Day Program.

Jaguar Series

JAGUAR

The Jaguar series focuses on advanced dragon coiling that integrates the lower cauldron, throat, and crown as one unit through the Fibonacci principle of internal torsion. This, in turn, empowers the toroidal field of the heart to expand beyond its known limits. A forward-thrusting, spiraling motion system containing compact, close-quarter gestures, Jaguar movements appear where you don't expect due to their uncanny speed.

Jaguar and Small Mountain: Twin Forms

The Jaguar and Small Mountain sequences introduce fast coiling methods that apply Lo Ban Pai principles into a martial format that is esoterically bound. It is the truest expression of the Tao. Tumultuous waters always find their rest within great depth.

Jaguar and Small Mountain are the twin reflection of heaven and earth integrating within the heart of man. One employs the torsion field and many applications of Mantis Fist, and the other utilizes the Hurricane fist as its primary modus operandi.

Traditionally taught and practiced individually to highlight and refine aspects of form, energy cultivation and perceptual speed, both Jaguar and Small Mountain cause the phenomenon of time-space displacement via the coiling motions. Once both sets have been assimilated individually, they are absorbed into the Three Treasures form and become amalgamated as one integral whole.

DYNAMIC APPLICATION
OF ENERGY CULTIVATION

The Jaguar series utilizes the principles of the Windlock system, Whispering Palms and the Three Treasures as its foundation. Thus, when the warrior begins the Jaguar series, the groundwork has been laid on many levels.

Windlock prepares the musculature, tendons, and ligaments while instilling optimized movement skills within a well-defined and contained area around the body.

Whispering Palms opens the meridian system – the electromagnetic pathways of the body – and supports the development of high-level, applied awareness both in stillness and in motion.

The Three Treasures unifies the potency of the three cauldrons to generate internal stability, cohesion, and abundance in terms of one's perceptual capacity to unify all forms of separatism within one's self.

SHADOW FIST KUNG FU PRINCIPLES

The Jaguar employs the graceful coiling movements of Spiral Energetics at full speed. It is the first of two foundation sets in the close-quarter combat skills of Lo Ban Pai. This training covers many levels and topics, including:

- Mastering timing and momentum, as spiraling movements, transition into explosive energetic applications and return back into complex dragon coiling sequences.

- Changing between left and right while maintaining flow as specific gathering gestures enliven gravitational forces that lie dormant in the left and right sides of the physical body.

- Torsion field sequences that generate potency within one's personal power while absorbing the incoming force of the electromagnetic potential surrounding the body.

- The application of the shadowless elbow to create cone-like vortexes that subtly interrupt the present time-space continuum. This allows the practitioner intimate glimpses into the unknown, whilst in the midst of dynamic action.

ADAPTATION AND FORMLESSNESS

Practicing the Jaguar Series opens energy channels that give rise to spontaneous realizations. This awareness is governed by formlessness yet adapts into the form that is required based on the frequential exchange presented in one's living circumstances.

In this program the initiate will awaken to their ability to flow with what is required in each situation. The intricate and advanced receptive faculties of your neural network will be activated. This is truly the inherent magic of Lo Ban Pai.

SPIRITUALITY AND BODY CONSCIOUSNESS

The human form can be utilized as a vehicle towards spiritual enlightenment. However, its purpose is often misunderstood or a subject of theoretical discussion, rather than functional application.

The Jaguar Series develops specific skills through powerfully applied movements that open the physical gateways to quantum realities. It involves the development of refined awareness in areas like speed and the application of silence whilst in motion, as well as feeling, trusting and following the body.

QUANTUM UNIVERSAL AWARENESS

These movements serve as a gateway to awaken the warrior to their dreaming awareness as a tool that can be applied in daily life. The outcome of a disciplined practice of the Jaguar Series is an increase in lucidity that allows the seer to access external visual imagery as composites of data that are usually out of the range of human perception.

Each reality that we become aware of through the practice of Lo Ban Pai reveals unique aspects of the individual's signature applied to that communion. When the initiate accesses these portholes, interdimensional phase-shifting occurs and information is then absorbed. In this process, the seer's resonant field morphs and energetically reflects its own findings through the practitioner's personal communion, which conversely will affect the world at large.

www.parallelperception.com

SMALL MOUNTAIN

SMALL MOUNTAIN

Small Mountain completes the trinity begun by the Three Treasures. A dynamic combat set that is paired with the Jaguar series and adds straight line thrusting applications, this vital practice develops focus and third eye awareness applied in immediate recapitulation, or direct knowing.

Incorporating blunt force and heavy electromagnetic impulses, it develops the potency of one's personal gravity in terms of its outward expression manifesting as propulsive impact. Upon integration of this set, consciousness shifts from one level to another very quickly.

SMALL MOUNTAIN AND JAGUAR: TWIN FORMS

The Jaguar and Small Mountain sequences introduce fast coiling methods that apply Lo Ban Pai principles within a martial format that is esoterically bound. It is the truest expression of the Tao. Tumultuous waters always find their rest within great depth.

Jaguar and Small Mountain forms are the twin reflection of heaven and earth integrating within the heart of man. One employs the torsion field and many applications of Mantis Fist, and the other utilizes the Hurricane Fist as its primary modus operandi.

Traditionally taught and practiced individually to highlight and refine aspects of form, energy cultivation and perceptual speed, both Jaguar and Small Mountain cause the phenomenon of time-space displacement via the coiling motions. Once both sets have been assimilated individually, they are absorbed into the Three Treasures form and become amalgamated as one integral whole.

HURRICANE FIST AND
ENERGETIC VORTICES

Small Mountain is a rapid coiling set with a focus on applying power in straight-line thrusting movements combined with the shadowless elbow. Powerfully positioned in front of the center of the solar plexus, these physical placements strengthen the willpower and determination of the practitioner.

This form adopts slow oscillating movements that create a gyroscopic effect within the central axis whilst maintaining a strongly grounded foundation. This renders the practitioner unpredictable for an opponent, not too dissimilar to a drop of water that lands on a spinning top and cannot find traction.

The main differences between the Jaguar Series and Small Mountain is that the latter employs a unique gateway that is generated by the hurricane fist. This technique is married with the shadowless elbow to create twin cone-like vortices that subtly displace the time-space continuum. These miniature torsion fields, or etheric mandalas, allow the warrior retrospective glimpses into the unknown.

SMALL MOUNTAIN MARTIAL EXPRESSION

Small Mountain adds the element of an explosive force within its application. This energy comes from an advantageous position created by dominating the bridge through blocking, deflecting or locking the opponent. The shadowless elbow appears and disappears unexpectedly, which increases the power of the trapping, stripping and locking applications that follow it. Lujan will meticulously explain each of these techniques and principles as they are introduced.

While the Jaguar has a wide view or awareness – like radar – Small Mountain adds a component of direct laser focus that explodes out of coiling and back again. The speed at which this switch takes place, when first experienced, seems astounding and is a testament to how this skill is built up in preparation phases.

EMPATHIC ATTUNEMENT

Even though this is a martial set, its primary emphasis – as for everything in Lo Ban Pai – is on the growth of one's perception into heightened realities that reveal the unfolding labyrinth that is our attention as beings upon an evolutionary path.

Small Mountain enhances focus within the midst of its complexity. This builds on the foundation of the Jaguar, which empowers a scanning awareness that can now dart instant flashes of insight to the warrior.

At this stage of training Lujan always emphasizes stillness within motion, for the application of knowledge is empty if one does not embody wisdom.

5 Day Program

PRIMORDIAL SHEN GONG:

JING CULTIVATING
SEXUAL ENERGY PRACTICE

PRIMORDIAL SHEN GONG:

Primordial Shen Gong refines the innate capacity to be empathically attuned to all beings, which also expands one's ability to move beyond the boundaries of the physical body. This precious jewel greatly enhances personal power and longevity.

This rejuvenating practice contains powerful techniques of Lo Ban Pai for sexual energy cultivation to enhance the primordial essence, which promotes physical strength and clarity. The entire sequence focuses upon Jing, Chi and Shen combined as a unified force, and the advanced principles of Shen application.

This heightened awareness of electromagnetic connectivity promotes the ability to align with a deep reservoir of sincerity within the self, which fosters the elusive state of communion with spirit.

JING CULTIVATION

Jing is the foundation energy cultivated in inner alchemy. Native to the lower dantien, it is the primal essence or life force that we inherit from our parents. While Jing can be used in martial arts, it is a key component of health and fuels clear, unimpeded perception at every level.

Primordial Shen Gong begins by addressing the principal necessity of fortifying and clearing this vital base of operations, which corresponds with the sexual center. The impact of Jing cultivation is palpable and students often describe their experience of feeling more present, grounded and powerful within just a few days of practice.

MANAGING INCREASED SEXUAL ENERGY: TAMING THE WILD-HORSE

Learning primordial energy cultivation techniques is advised under qualified supervision. Lujan explains this sensitive discipline clearly and meticulously, indicating how to calibrate training to harmonize the elements so as to build a stable base to support one's progress.

When sexual energy is cultivated without proper ethical practice it can easily rage out of control, hence the oriental term that refers to this phenomena as 'Wild-Horse'. Not only does Jing cultivation cease under these circumstances, leading to serious depletion of one's vital energy reserve, but the psychological effects of this volatile imbalance may lead to negative repercussions on those in one's environment.

LING KONG JING

Primordial Shen Gong also includes a component of Ling Kong Jing that trains the ability to project energy beyond the body. One key aspect is to lower one's center, which has everything to do with the grounding aspect of the practice. The principles of casting and toning, as taught in the Gravity series, are developed here.

Physical displacement phenomena may occur within a short time of applying these techniques and is even more likely to happen as empty force training matures. It may feel momentarily as if the world around you moves whilst you are standing still. This phenomenon is also often experienced when practicing the Jaguar Series.

ENERGETIC OUTCOMES OF THE PRACTICE

Sexual Cultivation Practice is far more complex than the name implies. Though it may indeed increase one's libido and help one experience a more fulfilling sex life, these are merely side-benefits and not the major focus.

It can take as little as a few days to experience Primordial Shen Gong adding a deeper and more tangible sense of gravity to every aspect of life. As energy levels rise dramatically, concentration becomes more focused and you will experience sensations of 'fullness' and being more 'earthed' as well as increased perceptual clarity.

JING AND EJACULATION

Taoist teachings maintain that too much ejaculation leads to poor health and a reduced life span. The emphasis placed upon retaining semen is due to the fact that it directly equates with Jing, or 'primordial essence', as described above.

Excess ejaculation consumes cerebrospinal fluid, which leads to brain shrinkage. Whereas a woman can have multiple climaxes without serious depletion of essence, a man cannot indulge in this without bearing the consequences sooner or later.

The force of Jing supplies energy to the lower three chakras, strengthens the legs and fosters a grounded sense of self. When Jing is abundant, this supplies Chi, and these two primordial energies join more easily and harmoniously together to combine into Shen. (see The Three Treasures program description for further information).

Eyes shine brightly as a sign of increased Shen and you will feel stronger as a result of developing deeper roots and a more stable base of power within your core.

STRENGTH, VIRILITY AND PERSONAL POWER

As we age, the vagina expands and the penis shrinks. These practices directly address this natural process and promote abundance of vital energy. The side-effects of this discipline include benefiting one's sex-life, especially in later years.

The vital health of a man's penis has a direct relationship to his physical and energetic strength. When correctly performed, these practices increase testosterone levels in a balanced way. Jing cultivation strengthens and enlarges the length and girth of the penis and tones the ligaments, activating synovial fluid and generating radiance via the fascial network.

Primordial Shen Gong practices allow energy to rise from the inguinal crease to the shoulder nest, which brings fullness to the internal channels. The lower dantien is intimately associated with this nerve complex via its connectivity to the sexual center. As these internal pathways fill with power and become as strong as steel bars and as elastic as a hose filled with pressurized water, qualities of uprightness, both physiologically and psychologically, are progressively upheld.

For anatomical reasons, the male version of this technique series differs from the female version. As a woman's genitalia points to the ground it is subject to gravity, and if this area is not kept toned, energy can leak from this vital center through neglect. The female practice addresses this by strengthening and tightening the vaginal complex and involves the use of a yoni egg crystal. This enlivens a very strong receptivity to the primal essence of the womb, this powerful sensorial base of operations that is a genetic blueprint that links to every woman that ever existed.

A man will develop their connectivity to the feeling center of the lower dantien through diligent practice of the rotational vortices within the Opening the Tao program. For those who are wondering, the training does not require disrobing, physical touch or anything similar.

PERSONAL DISCIPLINE AND FORTITUDE IN LIFE AND LOVE

As one practices self-regulation in one's sexual nature, and even learns how to enjoy sexual activity without physical release, this same quality of restraint and potency will naturally become available as a personal resource within every aspect of your life.

Loyalty – a deep ethical standpoint – must be maintained at the level of thoughts, visualizations and behavior. Tenderness, kindness and understanding through communication is one of the most important areas to uphold within this practice.

IMPORTANT NOTE

It bears reiterating that practitioners must be utterly dedicated to their ethical integrity in order to apply these techniques. This is not mere advice but a very strong warning.

Primordial Shen Gong is not for the faint-hearted, for without discipline this level of Jing cultivation can become extremely detrimental, and males, in particular, are especially vulnerable to serious imbalance when the potent fires of sexual energy are stoked.

If there is any incoherence on the level of loyalty, transparency, and care, every ounce of these issues will and must be drawn to the surface (which of course applies absolutely and equally to females as well). This practice can be devastating if love, kindness, and gentle forbearance are not brought into play. Engagement in this program entails a thorough reckoning with any submerged behaviors and attitudes and a cleansing of all that does not belong in a clear heart.

The prerequisite to do this program is the completion of the Initiation and Intermediate series. Available to approved students only.

5 Day Program.

Lo Ban Pai
Advanced Series

This series encompasses cultivation and full integration of all aspects of Lo Ban Pai, both for esoteric development and optionally for martial application. A highly advanced level that fuses the outer and inner realities into a seamless whole.

BINDING ROOTS
(INCLUDES TEMPLE BAGUA)

Binding Roots

This is a partially moving form that utilizes half-moon stepping. Elegant and intensely magnetic, it beckons the void that is behind the universal chi.

Binding Roots brings the cosmos into the temple of the body, whereby engaging with it one learns about the self through observing and experiencing the micro-macro interaction of the Tao expressing its mystery in every moment. The crowning jewel of the dynamic energy cultivation practices of the system, this form is a unique manifestation of the internal art of Lo Ban Pai.

Opening the Channels

This practice generates warmth and opens up the four major channels that run in unison through the arms and legs. As the stances apply pressure to the bones they become elastic and vibrant, yet as strong as flexible steel, creating power within the ligaments and tendons like tensile wire.

Martial Applications

Binding Roots will transfer all other forms from the Lo Ban Pai system into a moveable small space, creating explosive power that will build confidence and nurture the internal willpower through absorption of universal chi. It becomes a catalyst to translate all other intermediate sets into dynamic action.

It is a close-quarter, short-range system, whereby the stripping and locking capacity binds and gathers energy, then releases it as lightning force in a combat situation.

While the form reveals its beauty through the coiling movements, when applied they are highly effective as a self-defense mechanism, if necessary. When undertaking this program the student will also learn many of the principles and techniques of Shadow Fist Kung Fu.

TEMPLE BAGUA

Temple Bagua is incorporated in the Binding Roots program. This potent circular walking technique moves in intricate spirals that mimic the motions of celestial bodies within our universe. These movements integrate all knowledge learned in the introductory and intermediate programs. The training of the preceding forms cultivates hidden treasures. Once the initiate reaches this level, Lujan provides the keys to unlock these skills.

Temple Bagua is a unique expression of Lo Ban Pai and one of the crown jewels of the esoteric system that Lujan teaches. This Oriental shamanic movement set familiarizes the practitioner with the fundamentals of harnessing the power of focused chi before moving onto the refined expressions of this enigmatic universal force contained within its sister form, Plum Blossom.

YIN ENERGY CULTIVATION

The circular walking of Lo Ban Pai concentrates on the central force of the warrior, rather than an external central polestar focus, as is taught in many Bagua schools.

Similar techniques survive in various forms in Bon and some branches of Taoism and are best known in the West as the walking pattern for the martial art of Baguazhang. Lo Ban Pai's Temple Bagua is however fundamentally different from other expressions of the art.

This particular method enables the chi generated to be absorbed within the center of the warrior as they rotate. Additionally, by coiling partially inwardly and to the rear of the hip, the practitioner is familiarized with the essential energy that rises from the ground from this perspective. At this location there is a very powerful electromagnetic vortex, which is traditionally called 'witches broom'. The reason for this is that when the warrior contacts this area it has the shape of a dovetail, cascading from the back of the hips to the floor.

Pushing Hands

At the level of Binding Roots Lujan will teach a complex set of pushing hands that allows the vital chi to be released and re-circulated harmoniously, which in turn generates more power.

Telekinetic Skills

When Binding Roots is integrated with Temple Bagua it enhances connection with electric fibers that are subtly attached to the luminous cocoon, yielding the development of the phenomenon called Ling Kong Jing, which means 'empty force'. In other martial systems this technique is practiced with the primary focus on the empty force becoming controllable so as to be willfully applied.

In contrast, in Lo Ban Pai the mind is not employed, so this skill manifests as an energetic byproduct that is not connected to the desire of the practitioner. The student learns to focus this potency without desire so that it becomes an appropriate energetic response to circumstances. This practice delivers the initiate to an elusive state of awareness: a pure connection to spirit.

UNIQUE EXPRESSION OF CIRCLE WALKING

Circle walking mirrors the essential transit of planetary systems as a metaphor, typically with reference to a central point, or sun. Binding Roots turns this in on itself to bring the cosmos inside one's inner temple. By embodying these principles in motion, the initiate learns about the self through observing and experiencing the micro-macro interaction of the Tao expressing its mystery.

This interactive inner-alchemy represents an important paradigm shift in the way the body supports spiritual development. The net result of the spiraling practice of Lo Ban Pai creates dragon gates, which provides a direct, experiential link with eternity.

Level 1: 5 Days
Level 2: 5 Days
Complete Program: 10 Days

SHADOW FIST FUNDAMENTALS

SHADOW FIST FUNDAMENTALS

Shadow Fist Fundamentals introduces the initiate to the foundation of the Shadow Fist Kung Fu system of Lo Ban Pai.

This dynamic set of martial sequences incorporates simultaneous attack and defense reflexive routines that train the physiological neural net to respond with speed and efficiency and correspondingly develops power and directness within the mood of the warrior.

STATE OF NO MIND

In ancient times it was essential to have lightning reflexes that manifest before the mind realizes its outcome. The fighting art of Lo Ban Pai was used by master Lo Ban to protect himself while traveling the trade routes.

INTERNAL MARTIAL ART

The Shadow Fist system – or Black Fist as it was once known – deploys extremely advanced routines that set a precedent for a combined regimen that is applied to the esoteric field of the onslaught of an aggressor.

The effects of the sounds and impact of the blows that are employed confuses an attacker's neural net and creates an irreversible state of inertia that subdues their visual cortex for a few moments.

This is the reason why it was named Black Fist by those on the receiving end. It is of worthy of note to mention that the fundamentals of Shadow Fist Kung Fu are extremely advanced in comparison to other martial arts systems presently available.

PROTECTIVE FIELD

Shadow Fist is a perfect art for male and female practitioners for building power, confidence and an enduring, stable solar plexus that protects one's heart center. The techniques open the practitioner to enormous amounts of electromagnetic potential. It is a short, sharp and direct system of movement that fosters great fortitude and lightning-fast reflexes.

YIN CHI

In Shadow Fist Fundamentals the warrior will learn two sacred emperor stances plus martial routines – both mobile and static – that yield enormous amounts of power. These movements are developed by drawing upon the vast reservoirs of yin chi that have been cultivated through all the previous practices of Lo Ban Pai.

Even though the movements seem to be forceful and direct – or 'yang' – the primary force behind their impact is a very heavy electromagnetic reserve of yin chi that is accessed primarily through these two emperor poses.

COMMUNION WITH UNIVERSAL CHI

Shadow Fist routines can be trained every second day alternating with the Windlock system. These movements increase one's ability to absorb and manifest the yin energy that is produced by the earth and surrounds the practitioner as explosive power generated through the forearms and fists. This act in itself creates an everlasting communion with the planet.

They also foster health and promote longevity, supporting the warrior to rise every morning with vigor and unrelenting positivity for the activities of the oncoming day.

5 Day Program

PLUM BLOSSOM
AND THE WOODEN DUMMY

PLUM BLOSSOM

The Plum Blossom set is the culminating integration of the dynamic coiling motions, awakened energy and awareness cultivated through preceding practices. It expresses the heart of the warrior spirit actively – as a martial skill if required – but principally to provide energetic forbearance against the forces that seek to subdue one's unique expression.

This program also includes a form called Beautiful Springtime, which is an integral part of the short-force martial arts application taught in correspondence with the gateway to Shadow Fist Kung Fu.

GATEWAY TO SHADOW FIST KUNG FU

Plum Blossom is the gateway into Advanced Shadow Fist Kung Fu. As a dynamic walking form it integrates and applies previous learning through energized coiling and focused awareness, as a multi-level expression of the warrior spirit.

SHADOW FIST ORIGINS

Shadow Fist was traditionally known as 'Black Fist'. The reason for this mysterious name is that the shadow-less elbow and the slapping hands are so fast that the training partner (or opponent) will experience conscious blackout; and the only way to cope with this is to have the kinesthetic memory that causes one's creativity to harmonize with the onslaught, thereby protecting oneself. The art functions at close-quarter spacing and the straight-line stepping serves to define this range.

THE EIGHT DIRECTIONS OF THE BAGUA

The name Plum Blossom comes from the stepping path that describes a flower with eight petals spiraling out from the center to eight Gates. Building upon Temple Bagua foundations, The practitioner learns to absorb the centralized force and turn to face and walk in the eight specific locations of the outside of the Bagua circle, utilizing this energy to infuse one's outwardly facing mudras with power.

The set employs the principles of the Temple Bagua

walking and shifting, employing the unicorn and small twisting yang stance for rotations, returning to horse stance, then applying coiling straight-line techniques unique to Lo Ban Pai's Dragon Coiling System.

HARVESTING CHI

Plum Blossom is extremely energetic, teaching the practitioner to draw the coiling energy from the ground and environment to the forearms and palms.

As in Temple Bagua, the Plum Blossom practitioner acts from the center. The circle mirrors the containment area around the body – developed in Windlock and Shadow Fist Fundamentals – beyond which energy dissipates.

In practice any point can be the center, so the set cultivates the skill to make wherever the warrior is the central hub. This generates the potential necessary for the practitioner's personal power to be full and complete at each gateway that is faced, performing the guard-like gestures that protect the core.

The Heart Center

The center that is protected, and from which movements flow, is the heart. While some arts train the mind to harness and direct this energy, Plum Blossom expands the skill developed in Temple Bagua to respond to the environment following the dictates of the heart as opposed to the socialized mind.

The speed of awareness required to do this in daily life highlights the value of the skill the Plum Blossom teaches. Not only will the practitioner's responses be guided by the heart but such action will draw on personal power that is fully available to engage the experience – be it any normal life circumstance or encountering a dragon gate.

Beautiful Springtime
Partner Training Sequences

Beautiful Springtime introduces integral short-force martial applications of Lo Ban Pai, which are taught in correspondence with the Plum Blossom and the Wooden Dummy. This program includes instruction in pushing hands, coiling sticking hands, rolling sticking hands and various two-man sets.

Iron Oak Wooden Dummy

Wooden dummy sequences will be taught to cultivate the practitioner's ability to harness the power required to implement the straight-line techniques embedded within the dragon coiling.

Plum Blossom is only available to approved students that have completed the necessary prerequisites. This is a four-week program consisting of four levels, which can be undertaken as single weeks if preferred. This provides the student with the opportunity to learn the program in four separate 5-day sessions or attend a complete four-week course.

Level 1: 5 Days
Level 2: 5 Days
Level 3: 5 Days
Level 4: 5 Days
Complete Program: 20 Days

SHADOW FIST KUNG FU:
ADVANCED TECHNIQUES

Shadow Fist Kung Fu: Advanced Techniques

Shadow Fist fully articulates the internal principles of Lo Ban Pai as a formidable martial form. Powered by activated vortexes in the energy field, it is employed to fortify and shield the warrior while fully engaged in life and the pursuit of spiritual growth.

Incorporating sticking and pushing-hands, it includes exact translations of wooden dummy techniques into partner training routines. This was the art used to protect royalty, a testament to the possibilities of transforming energy cultivation into real-world application.

Protector of One's Sovereign Center

Shadow Fist Kung Fu is a very direct and formidable art form that was used to guard and protect the emperors of China. Once called 'Black Fist', it is the pinnacle martial application of Lo Ban Pai. Through performing Shadow Fist the warrior will ultimately be introduced to the latent potential that is stored within. This practice reinforces inherent willpower, which can then be applied to all facets of one's life.

PATH OF THE SPIRITUAL WARRIOR

All of the elements of Lo Ban Pai set the fundamental groundwork of energetics for Shadow Fist Kung Fu. Traditionally the practitioner is taught how to cultivate and generate chi before they learn to harness it, firstly as an internal reservoir of power and later as a martial skill.

Through Gravity, Opening the Tao, Awakening the Energy Body and the Windlock system the container of the physical and the etheric applications of the chi flow are operationally defined and developed to align the warrior's movements with their bioelectromagnetic potential.

Next, Dragon Coiling integrates the spiraling arm movements with the energetic template through Golden Lotus, Dragon's Tears and Whispering Palms. Then, Three Treasures, Jaguar, Small Mountain, Binding Roots, and Plum

Blossom techniques refine the now aligned gestures for more specific purposes, including the advanced martial applications within Lo Ban Pai.

Martial Applications

Shadow Fist is a close-quarter, short-force impact system with a speed of delivery that is immeasurable. It is precise, effective and unwavering, which is the reason why it was deployed to protect royalty.

The uncanny swiftness of Shadow Fist movements is facilitated by maintaining a tight frame of motion that coils along energetic paths natural to the body's architecture.

The system's coiling motions seamlessly explode into forward-thrusting attacks and back into the whirlwind flow again, as advancing footwork maintains and shortens the bridge to the opponent.

Protective Shield

The practice creates two forward-thrusting clockwise and anti-clockwise vortexes in front of the solar plexus and heart center. This forms a shield of protection for the seer and stabilizes the kinesthetic knowledge that has been developed from all previous movement forms that have been learned.

Many students ask how can they defend themselves from the onslaught of negativity and yet remain detached. Shadow Fist offers a way to be fully engaged, direct and confident while being guarded by the fortifying energetics created by this system.

FORTIFYING TECHNIQUES

• Wall bag skills to teach the practical application of the short-force method.

• Two-man set drills – sticking and pushing hands.

• Spontaneous reflex response training

• Development of internal energetics as a tool for focusing the short-force principle.

10 Day Program

SHAMANIC HEALING

Shamanic Healing

This is a bodywork and counseling program. During these one-on-one sessions Lujan will work on blockages held in the body and will assist in processing any emotional upheavals that occur. To actively engage in healing one's own imbalances is one of the most powerful gestures of service an individual can make. Guidance and support provided by Lujan is grounded in decades of experience as a healer, teacher and diligent practitioner of meditative and internal energy work.

HEALING THE BODY

Lujan is now offering private healing sessions utilizing a unique technique of holistic bodywork that originates in ancient Oriental medicinal wisdom. This method works directly on the luminous fibers that connect the energy body to the universe at large, activating the bioelectromagnetic fields that enhance life and awareness.

THE EMPATH'S ENERGY

During the healing sessions you will directly experience Lujan's personal power, which is felt as magnetic waves pulsating throughout your energy body. This transmission will allow you to achieve the inner silence that is necessary to attain the elusive state of heightened perceptual acuity that catalyzes true transformation.

Experiences can include visions and profound shifts into altered physiological consciousness, which opens the heart to its natural way of being. You will become aware of the movement of your life force within your luminous sphere as

Lujan realigns your energetic fibers via ligaments and tendons located in the back. You will also be instructed in specific techniques that enhance lucidity of perception, thereby enabling you to transform your viewpoint.

Empathic Attunement

Insights and advice pertaining to your developmental path is not governed by a pre-determined format but by a refined receptivity to the intricacies of your actual psychological and physiological blueprint. Non-judgmental and direct, Lujan's guidance is firmly oriented toward empowering a stance of full responsibility and ongoing personal development that leaves old patterning behind.

Intuitive Visions

In this program Lujan will demonstrate Dragon's Tears, using the power of this movement form to shift the gazer's attention. During this process you may experience visual anomalies and otherworldly phenomena. Lujan will also realign your chakra centers thus opening up ancient doorways of perception, enabling a direct experience of the unifying effects of truly present awareness as a unique connection to eternity.

PERSONAL POWER AND TRANSFORMATION

As Lujan accompanies you during these practices, he will assist you to process any upheavals that may arise so as to facilitate your growth of consciousness. The outcome is that you will be equipped to independently resolve any obstructions in your energy body. This will enable a complete and enduring healing that will be able to be sustained following the conclusion of the healing sessions.

TRANSFORMATIVE TECHNIQUES

The Healing Retreat includes empathic recapitulation practices, the Eight Gates of Dreaming Awake and the Healing Meditation.

5 Day Program

Practitioner Training Course
in Lo Ban Pai Bodywork

PRACTITIONER TRAINING COURSE
IN LO BAN PAI BODYWORK

In this course Lujan teaches a method of bodywork whereby the practitioner learns to proceed synchronistically in accordance with the energy grids that support and fortify the biofield.

During the lessons you will discover how to entrain your body to adapt to coiling spinning motions that are ambidextrously applied directly to connective tissue and ligaments that lift the fascia, allowing life force to flow harmoniously in and throughout the entire meridian system.

The practitioner will be able to apply the techniques over clothing or directly to the skin, both with and without oil.

THE EMPATHIC HEALER

As an initiate healer you will become increasingly aware of the profound effect of your presence within the company of your clients. Thus a journey begins that encompasses the tools that Lujan will guide you to utilize, as healers on your path to not only your own transformation but the transformation of those you come in contact with.

Lujan will teach all the necessary methods to help the practitioner utilize the empty hand principle: no mind, no imagery and no social projections in terms of expectations.

The process of becoming a healer entails an absolute and complete metamorphosis toward a state of clarity within the moment in order to bring about the necessary awareness that enables this sacred act to be performed. One's commitment to this work will boost emptiness into the elusive state of formlessness that creates immediate conductivity with the universe at large and allows the practitioner to become a pure conduit, thereby giving the ability to be of service to those who wish to receive absolute transmission.

MERIDIANS, PRESSURE POINTS AND CHI

The method of bodywork that Lujan teaches has its origins in the ancient healing arts of the Orient. Once the entire process is learnt the student will be taught how to adjust the duration time in accordance with the needs of their client, following a defined path that comprehensively addresses the entire meridian system, acupuncture points, connective tissues and fascia. By encouraging a free flow of blood and chi this method activates the endocrine system, and consequently stimulates a lymphatic cleansing that promotes the release of physical and emotional blockages.

LO BAN PAI MOVEMENT FORMS

For those who wish to undertake this course it is optional but highly recommended, in terms of production of energy, to practice Dragon's Tears and the Windlock System, in order to cleanse, strengthen and fortify the chakras and also replace the life-giving chi that one will invariably transmit through the practice of healing and empathic attunement.

HEALING GUIDANCE

Lujan will also teach the necessary etiquette that surrounds the conductivity that is to be one with the recipient so as to have the ability to see and act appropriately in accordance with their needs. Meditation techniques will also be taught that you may share with your clients.

Lujan will familiarize himself with the needs of the individual practitioners and appropriately deal with the obstacles that face them on their journey, so be prepared to expect the unexpected.

BECOMING A TRUE HEALER

It is not only a journey to learn to heal others; it is a path to discover the person you have never met and will never become familiar with once you reach a crucial threshold. There stands the true empath, on a flat-line reality that is so motionless that all motion is felt.

Practitioner Training Course in Lo ban Pai Bodywork is a two-week course and is limited to six students.

This button will be awarded to certified practitioners who complete the Practitioner Training Course in Lo Ban Pai Bodywork with Lujan Matus. It will link to a page to verify the names of all qualified practitioners. Please note that it is the responsibility of the practitioner to consult with the regulations of your country of residence in terms of what is required to practice as a healer.

THE BOOKS OF LUJAN MATUS

The unique teachings of Lujan Matus are a priceless resource of wisdom that pertain directly to human evolution. His responsibility to embody and transmit that legacy defines his purpose and is the driving force behind his work. As a teacher and guide, Lujan offers tools and techniques that allow you to recognize and develop your own personal relationship with the unknown. He embraces the all-encompassing view of empathy and compassion as the essential foundation of his philosophical approach.

Complex yet practical, each edition builds upon the

subtle framework defined by your own personal journey, in accordance with your life path. With each subsequent reading you will discover new aspects of your inner self and deepen your understanding of the very subtle application of empathic communion.

THE ART OF STALKING PARALLEL PERCEPTION

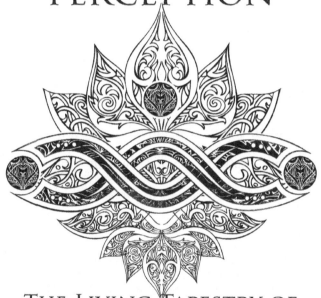

THE LIVING TAPESTRY OF
LUJAN MATUS

www.parallelperception.com

The Art of Stalking
Parallel Perception

The particular way in which this book impacts one's personal path is not easy to describe. What is conveyed here becomes so inexplicably intertwined with one's immediate reality, inner and outer, that once we come into contact with this information our own paradigm begins to shift, as previously undreamt of possibilities become increasingly apparent to us.

Essentially, this is a guide to activating our hidden reservoirs of multidimensional human potential. As we become immersed in Lujan's extraordinary life story, a wealth of encrypted knowledge is imperceptibly absorbed. Wellsprings of adaptive wisdom and pragmatic tools for self-liberation trigger a genuine awakening that can't be ignored.

Although the teachings outlined are very direct by nature, we find ourselves drawn back to these pages again and again to discover previously unnoticed layers of meaning. Even during the editing process, going over the same text dozens and dozens of times, I have been continually impacted to review and renew my understanding. My very molecules crave the authenticity of these teachings and the expansion they deliver.

To be part of making this information available to the world is an honor that I will always be grateful for, and not only because I value so deeply what Lujan has to offer. The process itself has been so intensely rewarding, challenging and incredibly synchronistic that it utterly confirms the ultra-dimensional consistency within what Lujan outlines, to a degree that defies explanation.

To complete this introduction, I asked Lujan to describe parallel perception for someone picking up this book for the first time, and this was his reply.

'Parallel perception refers to accessing alternate realities; time-space continuums that are simultaneously operational yet not linearly connected via the expectations of a social mind. These dimensional gateways are omnipresently available and eternally fluctuate as a quantum reflection upon our moments, those precious points of arrival that

175

continually escape us.'

Ten years since its original publication, the revised edition of The Art of Stalking Parallel Perception contains a treasure trove of new information that clarifies and expands upon central themes, presenting this timeless shamanic wisdom in a more accessible format. Amongst many other crucial additions, Lujan explains for the first time the workings of the mysterious energy double and how it manifests and connects to us in this world. We are introduced to the intricacies of seemingly indescribable interdimensional processes related to seeing, third-eye perception and the cyclic nature of time, as it exists within parallel continuums. These descriptions trigger realizations that tear the lid off the Pandora's box of human behavior and allow the light of clear perception to come streaming in.

This is more than a chronicle of someone else's journey. It is an invitation to fully engage with your own. Via an empowering sequence of events and conversations with enigmatic seers, we are introduced to the mechanisms and subtleties of the most elusive subjects pertaining to our human dilemma and reminded of the expanded possibilities that we

176

have lost sight of on the long road of human socialization.

By deftly weaving the luminous strands of our heart's remembrance, Lujan cuts through the veil of unwholesome socialization to reach into our deepest reservoirs of consciousness and remind us where we truly stand. Our living tapestry is alive and continuously unfolding, just as the holographic mystery of our existence is evolving in ways that cannot be anticipated, and which come to light differently for each of us. Lujan's journey plants jewels into one's cognitive system that irreversibly alter the equation and whose true worth will only be revealed by time's passing.

The Art of Stalking Parallel Perception
is available on Amazon and Audible.

www.parallelperception.com

Awakening the Third Eye

Discovering the True Essence of Recapitulation

Lujan Matus

Awakening the Third Eye

Our third eye is nothing less than a porthole to gnosis.

We have an inbuilt ability to access infinite wisdom that is absolutely pertinent to our lives yet is often inaccessible due to its enigmatic nature.

Glimpses of our universal connectivity come to us in subtleties, signs and intuitions that brush against us gently or urgently, bringing vital messages that link us to a larger arena of activity, relentlessly inviting us to become aware of our galactic context.

These are veiled communications from our third eye matrix. To cultivate receptiveness to this ongoing exchange is to travel into full remembrance of who we are.

This book offers invaluable insight into how to recognize and develop your own relationship with the magical faculty of third eye seeing and ways to integrate that into daily life practices.

Lujan Matus deftly ushers us into the heart of the mysteries of perception and consciousness, presenting new

www.parallelperception.com

perspectives on our place in the universe and what we are capable of. His teachings trigger welcome revolutions in consciousness and the many techniques he gives here are powerful tools for personal transformation. Amongst those techniques are exercises for becoming aware of the blue spectrum, the highest vibration of light, where all manner of energetic activity is taking place in an eternally fluctuating exchange. Developing the capacity to perceive that luminous interactivity reveals a magical aspect of seeing which inevitably becomes a conduit to a new way of being.

This publication broadens the bandwidth, illuminating with dimensional yet practical information and clearly indicating an entry point into parallel perceptions, possibilities, and potentialities such as we have only dreamed of.

Awakening the Third Eye

is available on Amazon and Audible.

Shadows in the Twilight

Conversations with a Shaman

Lujan Matus

www.parallelperception.com

SHADOWS IN THE TWILIGHT

When W. L. Ham approaches the Nagual Lujan Matus for insight into enigmatic events that have marked his awareness, what he learns revolutionizes everything he thought he knew. Realizing he has found an authentic guide, Bill enters into an intensive apprenticeship and directly begins to experience our living matrix as the multiplex of lucid interactivity that it truly is.

Like countless others, Bill had been galvanized when concepts like the *Energy Double, Dreaming Awareness* and *First* and *Second Attention* were introduced in the 1960s by Carlos Castaneda. Exploring these fascinating propositions in his own waking and dreaming life, he found himself faced with discoveries and challenges utterly unaccounted for by conventional definitions of reality.

What began as a faithful documenting of question and answer sessions has resulted in a most extraordinary manual on the crucial yet little understood subject of reclaiming our transdimensional sovereignty. A friendly flow of dialogue belies the gravity of this material, as Lujan deftly elucidates the very fabric of existence with humble yet compelling authority.

These are no second-hand sorcery tales but genuine revelations from a seer bound by his inevitability to communicate what he knows. Describing the innermost workings of the holographic universe with a rare precision, these teachings decode riddles of perception that have long been surrounded with confusion, providing a luminous bridge to our true potential as human beings. Although what Lujan reveals is sometimes alarming, this is tempered by his multifaceted affirmation that the key to freedom lies in sincerely applying ourselves to the moment that continually escapes us; guided only by that most precious instrument of divination, our heart.

Shadows in the Twilight
is available on Amazon and Audible.

WHISPERINGS OF THE DRAGON

SHAMANIC TECHNIQUES
TO AWAKEN YOUR PRIMAL POWER

LUJAN MATUS

www.parallelperception.com

WHISPERINGS OF THE DRAGON

The revolution begins within, and this is a step-by-step guide to setting your personal metamorphosis in motion, effective immediately.

Lujan Matus reveals here, in clear and accessible language, how to recover your authentic self, using the simplest yet most profoundly useful techniques you could ever apply.

Complex processes of socialization distance us from our original essence very early on in our formation. Our socio-cultural inheritance weighs heavily on our intangible self and is reflected in an erosion of trust in our intuitive knowing and a consequent inability to see and do what is truly necessary.

This dilemma of conditioning, no matter where we are from and however aware we become of its intricacies, cannot be addressed by merely thinking about it.

A complete turnaround is required. Restoring our natural state of inner silence, that elusive axis of enlightenment, is our golden key to personal and collective freedom, and providing a precise and practical way to do that is exactly what this book achieves.

Your journey through the Eight Gates of Dreaming Awake will open the door for your primal essence to return to your present moment continuum. This book delivers ancient shamanic wisdom and quantic insights that allow precious points of arrival to be sustained within the power of one's omnipresence.

The techniques in this book can be successfully applied to any ideology, religion or philosophy.

Whisperings of the Dragon
is available on Amazon and Audible.

WHO AM I?

AN IN-DEPTH GUIDE TO
EMPATHIC COMMUNION

LUJAN MATUS

www.parallelperception.com

Who am I?

Who am I, if not my heart?

A close encounter with the mysterious force field universally known as the white light, triggers a series of catalytic awakenings that deliver radical insights into what it means to be alive. In sharing these revelatory seeds of consciousness, Lujan Matus invites us to openly examine bias and discover where our alignments are leading us.

Incalculable variables of vibration define our reality from A to Z. In a rapidly changing technological and social context, it is now time we took a very close look at the pervasive influence of frequency upon our perception and behavior, both individually and collectively.

To be governed by heart awareness within our personal application to the world is how we can reassign our attention to what actually matters. Pure feeling guides us into our innate ability to infuse with one another to the point where we experience unified consciousness. Full remembrance of this empathic communion is an evolutionary imperative whose

www.parallelperception.com

time has come.

Authenticity and taking the risk to truly care are not only crucial to our survival but necessary traits indicating readiness to participate in the greater galactic community. Beyond our earthly holding zone communication is sent and received as direct energetic transmissions that transcend cultural or species-based codes and boundaries. Truth and sincerity is the only currency that has value, and nothing less will open this elusive door.

By introducing perspectives that enable us to look beyond the thresholds we are contained within, this book shines a powerful light upon the lies and limitations that have been perpetuated towards humankind. Controversial and necessary, these internal illuminations have the power to change the world, for they will change you. Are you ready? You've only your illusions to lose.

Who am I?
is available on Amazon and Audible.

ORACLE OF THE HEART

WHISPERINGS OF WISDOM
FOR DAILY REFLECTION

LUJAN MATUS

www.parallelperception.com

THE ORACLE OF THE HEART

Open up these pages randomly

and discover yourself within their meanings.

The purpose of an oracle is to openly reveal information within the reservoirs of one's own inspiration. Trust yourself to respond to the mechanisms of no mind that will arise through the process of your heartfelt feelings coming upon you. Engaging within this reflective mirror will unveil the clarity of your life path as it continually unfolds within your daily practices of sincerity. The Oracle can be consulted diligently on a regular basis or whenever you feel the need to explore.

www.parallelperception.com

NEW TITLES BY LUJAN MATUS
COMING SOON:

THE POWER OF EMPTINESS
BEING, KNOWING AND NOT-DOING

LUJAN MATUS

THE TRUTHS OF JESHUA
AN INTERPRETATION OF THE GOSPEL OF THOMAS

LUJAN MATUS

www.parallelperception.com

AS I AM,
SO ARE OTHERS;
AS OTHERS ARE, SO AM I;
HAVING THUS IDENTIFIED
SELF AND OTHERS,
HARM NO ONE NOR
HAVE THEM HARMED.

BUDDHA

For information regarding workshops
and private tuition with Lujan Matus please visit:

www.parallelperception.com

Made in the USA
Las Vegas, NV
15 January 2023

65662112R00121